Philosophy and the Scienc

What is the origin of our universe? What are dark matter and dark energy? What is our role in the universe as human beings capable of knowledge? What makes us intelligent cognitive agents seemingly endowed with consciousness? Scientific research across both the physical and cognitive sciences raises fascinating philosophical questions. *Philosophy and the Sciences for Everyone* introduces these questions and more. It begins by asking what good is philosophy for the sciences, before examining the following topics:

- the origin of our universe
- dark matter and dark energy
- anthropic reasoning in philosophy and cosmology
- evolutionary theory and the human mind
- consciousness
- intelligent machines and the human brain
- embodied cognition.

Designed to be used on the corresponding Philosophy and the Sciences online course offered by the University of Edinburgh this book is also a superb introduction for anyone looking for a concise overview of key themes in philosophy of science and popular science.

Michela Massimi, David Carmel, Andy Clark, Jane Suilin Lavelle, John Peacock, Duncan Pritchard, Alasdair Richmond, Peggy Seriès, Kenny Smith and **Mark Sprevak** are all based at the University of Edinburgh, UK.

Philosophy and the Sciences for Everyone

Edited by
Michela Massimi

David Carmel
Andy Clark
Jane Suilin Lavelle
John Peacock
Duncan Pritchard
Alasdair Richmond
Peggy Seriès
Kenny Smith
Mark Sprevak

 Routledge
Taylor & Francis Group

LONDON AND NEW YORK

Philosophy and the Sciences

THE UNIVERSITY of EDINBURGH

EIDYN
EDINBURGH CENTRE
FOR EPISTEMOLOGY
MIND · NORMATIVITY

Taught by Dr. Michela Massimi, Dr. David Carmel, Professor Andy Clark, Dr. Jane Suilin Lavelle, Professor John Peacock, Professor Duncan Pritchard, Dr. Alasdair Richmond, Dr. Peggy Seriès, Dr. Kenny Smith, Dr. Mark Sprevak, Professor Barbara Webb

This completely free and open online course will introduce you to some of the main areas and topics at the key juncture between philosophy and the sciences. Each week a philosopher and a scientist will jointly introduce you to these important questions at the forefront of scientific research: What is the origin of our universe? What are dark matter and dark energy? What is our role in the universe as human agents capable of knowledge? What makes us intelligent cognitive agents seemingly endowed with consciousness?

We will explain the science behind each topic in a simple, non-technical way, while also addressing the philosophical and conceptual questions arising from it. Areas you'll learn about will include:

- **Philosophy of cosmology**, where we'll consider questions about the origin and evolution of our universe, the nature of dark energy and dark matter and the role of anthropic reasoning in the explanation of our universe.
- **Philosophy of psychology**, among whose issues we will cover the evolution of the human mind and the nature of consciousness.
- **Philosophy of neurosciences**, where we'll consider the nature of human cognition and the relation between mind, machines and the environment.

Watch an intro video and sign up for the course at
https://www.coursera.org/course/philsci

This edition published 2015
by Routledge
2 Park Square, Milton Park, Abingdon, Oxon OX14 4RN

Simultaneously published in the USA and Canada
by Routledge
711 Third Avenue, New York, NY 10017

Routledge is an imprint of the Taylor & Francis Group, an informa business

British Library Cataloguing in Publication Data
A catalogue record for this book is available from the British Library

Library of Congress Cataloging in Publication Data
Philosophy and the sciences for everyone / by Michela Massimi
[and 9 others].
pages cm
Includes bibliographical references and index.
1. Science–Philosophy. I. Massimi, Michela.
Q175.P51216 2015
501–dc23
2014024531

ISBN: 978-1-138-785441 (hbk)
ISBN: 978-1-138-785434 (pbk)
ISBN: 978-1-315-767772 (ebk)

Typeset in Times New Roman
by Taylor & Francis Books

Printed and bound by CPI Group (UK) Ltd, Croydon, CR0 4YY

Contents

Preface

For centuries, philosophy and the sciences have gone hand in hand. Throughout the seventeenth and the eighteenth centuries, 'natural philosophy' provided the blueprint for modern physics, chemistry, astronomy, no less than botany and medicine. Newton, for example, called his masterpiece *Mathematical Principles of Natural Philosophy,* and philosophical reflections about the nature of space and time played a central role in Newton's physics. In the eighteenth century, Kant's philosophical speculations about the origins of the universe led him to the nebular hypothesis, later developed by Laplace as one of the first attempts at a modern scientific explanation in cosmology. But what good is philosophy for the sciences? And what can contemporary philosophers learn from the sciences? While still at the beginning of the twentieth century, philosophy had a profound influence on the discoveries of Einstein, Bohr, and other pioneers of the time, it might seem that the dialogue between philosophy and the sciences has come to an end. After all, we live in an era where scientific research is so specialized, diversified, and run on such a large scale that – the sceptics argue – there is very little that philosophy can contribute to contemporary science.

This book is our modest attempt at proving the sceptics wrong. The dialogue between philosophy and the sciences has never been richer, more pervasive, and timely. What is the origin of our universe? What are dark matter and dark energy, and what reasons do we have for believing in their existence? Is the universe such as to allow life to evolve? Has the human mind evolved as a series of 'mini-computers', adapted to solve problems that our ancestors faced? And to what extent, is our mind – in its functioning – like a computer? What makes us conscious human beings? And what role do technology and environment play in understanding how our minds work? These are central, timely, and cutting-edge questions in contemporary science that will occupy us in the course of this book – as a journey from the cosmos, to consciousness, and computers.

Of course, this selection of topics is not intended to be a comprehensive or exhaustive introduction to the many ways in which philosophy and the sciences (broadly construed) are still engaged in a mutually beneficial dialogue (we would need a much bigger book for that). Instead, we selectively focus on some timely topics in the philosophy of the physical sciences, and the philosophy of cognitive sciences, with the hope of probing each of them a little bit deeper than a whistle-stop tour through the sciences, broadly construed, would have allowed.

Hence the book is structured in two parts. In the first part we focus on three key issues in contemporary philosophy of cosmology. We start in Chapter 1 with a general introduction to philosophy of science. We take you through the famous relativist debate about Galileo and Cardinal Bellarmine. You will learn about what makes scientific knowledge 'special' compared with other kinds of knowledge, the importance of demarcating science from non-science, and how philosophers such as Popper, Duhem, Quine, and Kuhn came to answer these questions. In Chapters 2, 3, and 4 we turn to a particular branch of philosophy of science, called philosophy of cosmology. This is a burgeoning field at the key juncture of philosophy of science and cutting-edge research in cosmology. Chapter 2 is dedicated to the origins of our universe and provides a general overview of the history of cosmology and of the philosophical problems (laws, uniqueness, observability) that stood in the way of cosmology becoming a science in its own right (from being a branch of metaphysics, back in the eighteenth century). In Chapter 3, we discuss the current cosmological model, which talks about dark matter and dark energy: we ask what dark energy and dark matter are, what the evidence for them is, and which rival theories are currently available. This will provide us with an opportunity to explore a well-known philosophical problem known as underdetermination of theory by evidence. Next, in Chapter 4, we ask the question of why our universe seems to be such as to allow life to have evolved, according to the anthropic principle. We clarify what the anthropic principle says, and how these philosophical reflections may or may not find a counterpart in inflationary cosmology and the hypothesis of a multiverse.

After these chapters on philosophy of cosmology, we turn our attention to philosophy of cognitive sciences. This is a thriving area where philosophers of mind, cognitive scientists, psychologists, and linguists are joining forces to provide a better grasp of how the human mind has evolved and how it functions. We start in Chapter 5, with a fascinating journey through evolutionary psychology and the debate about nativism: we look at examples coming from ecology, such as beavers' colonies, to understand how the human mind might have adapted to solve specific tasks that our ancestors faced. In Chapter 6, we zoom in on the actual functioning of the human mind as a computer able to perform computations, and we look at the scientific ideas behind the mind–computer analogy. Chapter 7 takes us through cutting-edge research in psychology on the nature of consciousness, and pressing issues such as the role of consciousness in the vegetative state and other syndromes. Finally, in Chapter 8, we review the state of the art in the blossoming area of 'embodied cognition'. This is a recent trend that has brought to the general attention the importance of going beyond the 'neurocentric' view of how our mind works, and re-evaluating the central role of technology and environment in developing our cognitive capacities.

This book has been written for anyone who may be interested in learning about philosophy of science, not from the point of view of the history of the subject and its internal debates (there are plenty of excellent introductions already available on this). Instead, this book gives you an introduction to philosophy of science by exploring cutting-edge debates between philosophers and scientists on timely topics, such as dark matter and dark energy, mind and machines, consciousness, and evolutionary psychology. As such, we aim to offer an accessible, non-technical introduction to each topic, without presupposing too much background knowledge in either philosophy or science. Each chapter has a summary, list of study questions, further readings (both introductory and advanced) as well as internet resources. Key terms are emphasized in bold and defined in the glossary at the end of the book.

In the spirit of fostering dialogue between philosophy and the sciences, each chapter has been jointly written by a philosopher and a scientist. The process of jointly writing each of these chapters has been a rewarding journey for all of us, and I'd like to thank all the contributors for seeing this journey through: David Carmel (Psychology), Andy Clark (Philosophy of Cognitive Sciences), Jane Suilin Lavelle (Philosophy), John Peacock (Physics and Astronomy), Alasdair Richmond (Philosophy), Peggy Seriès (Informatics), Kenny Smith (Linguistics), and Mark Sprevak (Philosophy). Special thanks to James Collin for precious help with the copy-editing of the volume. I hope you will find the journey through the book as rewarding as we did!

This book is born out of a free and open-source MOOC ('massive open online course'), called 'Philosophy and the Sciences' and offered through the University of Edinburgh, following the success of our first MOOC 'Introduction to Philosophy' and associated book *Philosophy for Everyone.* The MOOC 'Philosophy and the Sciences' is to be launched in October 2014, with eight-week video lectures, forum discussions, and online self- and peer-assessment. I'd like to thank the University of Edinburgh for the institutional support in making possible this cross-College interdisciplinary collaboration. I want to thank especially the Principal, Professor Sir Timothy O'Shea, for enthusiastically supporting the project from the start; the Vice-Principal, Jeff Hayward; the Head of the College of Humanities and Social Science, Dorothy Miell; the Head of the College of Science and Engineering, Lesley Yellowlees; the Head of the School of Philosophy, Psychology, and Language Sciences, Andy McKinlay, and the School Administrator, Debbie Moodie; and the whole MOOCs Vice-Principal's Office, with Amy Woodgate, Lucy Kendra, Scott Imogen, and Nicol Craig for kindly assisting us every step of the way in the MOOC. The course will have several iterations, so if you have come to this book in some non-MOOC-related way, you may be interested in enrolling in our MOOC. A very warm welcome to everyone from the team of Philosophy and the Sciences!

Michela Massimi

1 What is this thing called science?

A very brief philosophical overview

Michela Massimi and Duncan Pritchard

What is science? Evidence, knowledge claims, and their justification

Scientific inquiry is widely considered to be a paradigmatic way of acquiring knowledge about the world around us. But what is science? And what makes scientific knowledge 'special', compared with other kinds of knowledge (see Achinstein 2010; Chalmers 1999; Goldacre 2009)? Here is one possible answer to this question: science just is what people who are professional scientists (e.g. in university science departments, or in the scientific research wings of large corporations, and so on) do. So, for example, astrology, which is not practised by professional scientists (but by e.g. newspaper columnists), is not a science, whereas astronomy, which is practised by professional scientists, is. A moment's reflection should reveal that this isn't a particularly helpful account of what science is.

For example, couldn't someone undertake a scientific inquiry and yet be an amateur, and so not be part of any professional scientific community? Moreover, do all the inquiries undertaken by professional scientists as part of their work count as scientific inquiries? Note that even the contrast between astronomers and astrologists isn't all that helpful in this regard once we inspect it more closely. There are *professional* astrologers after all, and such people may be regarded by themselves and those around them (e.g. their clients) as bona fide scientists. We clearly need to dig a little deeper.

In order to bring our question into sharper relief, consider the well-known Bellarmine–Galileo controversy about the validity of Ptolemy's geocentric system vs Copernicus's heliocentric system. This historical episode is well documented, and it has been the battleground of important discussions about what epistemologists call *epistemic relativism*, namely the view that norms of reasoning and justification for our knowledge claims seem to be relative (see Rorty 1979; Boghossian 2006). Epistemic relativism contends that while there might well be facts of the matter about whether or not our planetary system is indeed heliocentric, it does not follow that heliocentrism is the most rational view to believe. The epistemic relativist would contend that to assess the disagreement between Galileo and Bellarmine on whether or not the Earth moves, one would need to assess the epistemic standards and norms at work in assessing such claims. But the problem is that Galileo and Bellarmine used two seemingly incompatible norms or epistemic principles to evaluate the truth of their respective claims. While Galileo relied on the observational evidence coming from his telescope, Cardinal Bellarmine relied on the testimony of the Bible. In other words, Galileo and Bellarmine appealed to two different epistemic principles for the justification of their respective beliefs (Boghossian 2006, chs 5 and 6). Galileo appealed to the epistemic principle, which might be called *observation* whereas Bellarmine resorted to the epistemic principle of *revelation*. The former roughly says that given the telescopic evidence that Galileo had available at his time, if it seemed to Galileo that the Earth moved around the sun, then Galileo was justified in believing that the Earth moved around the sun. The latter principle, by contrast, says that given the testimony of the Bible as the revealed word of God, if it seemed to Bellarmine that the Earth was at rest in the centre of the universe, then Bellarmine was justified in believing that the Earth was at rest in the centre of the universe.

The epistemic relativist relies here on a powerful argument, known as the 'no neutral ground' argument (see Siegel 2011). The 'no neutral ground' argument claims that there was no common ground or neutral standard that Galileo and Bellarmine shared at the time and which could be used unambiguously to discern who was right and who was wrong. More precisely, to ascertain whether one of them was in fact wrong, one would need to offer reasons and arguments for proving that the epistemic principle of observation is in fact superior to Bellarmine's epistemic principle of revelation. Can such reasons and arguments be found?

A Galilean supporter may easily invoke here the reliability of the telescope and telescopic evidence in justifying Galileo's beliefs. The telescope was a scientific instrument that could be deployed to test the Copernican hypothesis and confront it directly with *observational* evidence. The evidence from the Bible for the geocentric hypothesis was of an altogether different kind: it was *textual* evidence, based on the authority of the Bible as the revealed word of God. So it may seem that the superiority of observational evidence over textual evidence can speak in favour of the superiority of Galileo's observation over Bellarmine's epistemic principle of revelation.

Not so fast. For one thing, it is not immediately obvious why *textual* evidence should be per se inferior to *observational* evidence. Think of the human sciences, and disciplines such as archaeology or anthropology where textual evidence (or oral evidence by members of a community) is routinely used to justify claims that we believe to be correct about the past, or about cultural practices. For sure, there are contexts in which *textual* evidence is the primary kind of evidence available to justify knowledge claims (in archaeology or anthropology) that we are inclined to think of as valid and scientific. But there is more. Back at the time of Galileo, the observational evidence delivered by the telescope was itself the object of acrimonious controversy. Not everyone at the time believed that the telescope was reliable or that telescopic evidence should have the upper hand over textual evidence from the Bible. Indeed, the scientific status of telescopic evidence was as much at stake in this debate as was the belief in heliocentrism.

To start, Galileo did not have a full-blown optical theory to explain how his telescope worked or whether it was reliable, although he did have a *causal explanation* about how the lens of the telescope worked in making the celestial objects appear more similar to the way they are in nature. However, Galileo's opponents endorsed the opposite causal explanation about the working of the telescope, whose lens – they thought – magnified and distorted the actual size of celestial objects. Galileo's foes, from Christopher Clavius to Lodovico delle Colombe and Cesare Cremonini, objected to the reliability of the telescope on the ground that it did not seem to magnify the stars, by contrast with other celestial objects: the size of the stars appeared to be the same to the naked eye and to the telescope. At stake in this debate was the issue of whether or not the halos of the stars visible to the naked eye should be taken or not taken into account in the estimate of their actual size: Aristotelians such as Horatio Grassi thought that it should, while Galileo thought that it should not, because it was illusory. The debate was sparked when Grassi (under the pseudonym of Lothario Sarsi) published this objection in his 1619 *Libra astronomica,* which Galileo rebutted in *The Assayer.* The final verdict went to Galileo because the scientific community eventually embraced Galileo's causal explanation of how the telescope worked and why it was reliable. To use Rorty's expression, we all stand on the grid that Galileo established with his victory.

This historical example illustrates the epistemic relativist's 'no neutral ground' argument, and the difficulty of identifying a common ground or a common measure to assess and evaluate knowledge claims in their historical context. But there is a further, stronger argument that relativists can use against the claim of universally valid norms of reasoning in science. This is called the 'perspectival argument' (see Siegel 2011), and it says that given the contextual and historically situated nature of our scientific knowledge, it follows that what we can know (what is both true and justified to believe) depends inevitably on the perspective of the agent. Leaving aside for now the issue of how we should think of or define a perspective – either in terms of the system of beliefs endorsed by the agent (see Sosa 1991); or in terms of the hierarchy of scientific models defining a scientific perspective (see Giere 2006) – the important issue for our discussion here is that if the perspectival argument is correct, then our knowledge claims are bound or determined by the perspective of the agent so that again there are no universal norms or standards to evaluate those knowledge claims *across different perspectives.*

We cannot enter here into the details of the debate surrounding epistemic relativism and its far-reaching implications for science and scientific knowledge (see Kusch 2002). Instead, we simply want to draw attention to what is at stake in this debate, namely the notions of truth and scientific progress. If the epistemic relativist is correct in the 'no neutral ground' argument and the 'perspectival argument', one may legitimately conclude that scientific inquiry should not be regarded as an endeavour to gain an increasingly better, and more likely to be true knowledge of the universe we live in. For there are no universal norms of reasoning or standards to which we can appeal in evaluating knowledge claims and we are trapped into the strictures of our respective perspectives. If this is indeed the case, how can science progress? And is there any goal at all at the end of scientific inquiry? Truth, as correspondence with the way things are in nature, would be a natural candidate goal for scientific inquiry: we expect our scientific theories to improve on their predecessors, to show why their predecessors were successful to the extent that they were, and to extend the range of phenomena that could be explained and predicted over and above those of their predecessors. In other words, if truth is the ideal goal of scientific inquiry, we could take the history of science as a progressive sequence of scientific theories, which were more and more likely to be true, while also fallible and revisable. The view of science that takes truth as the final aim of scientific theories is known as **scientific realism** and it goes right against epistemic relativism in claiming that there must be universal norms of reasoning and standards through which we can assess knowledge claims and discern scientific ones (e.g. Galileo's belief in heliocentrism) from pseudo-scientific ones (such as Bellarmine's belief in geocentrism). In the rest of this chapter we will look at a prominent attempt to identify a universal scientific method able to discern science from pseudo-science, in Karl Popper's view. Next, we will look at how some of the aforementioned relativist intuitions found their way again into the debate on the scientific method (or lack thereof) in the works of Duhem, Quine, and Kuhn.

From inductivism to Popper's falsification

Philosophers of science are interested in understanding the nature of scientific knowledge and its distinctive features, compared with other forms of knowledge (say, knowledge by testimony). For a very long time, they strove to find what they thought might be the distinctive method of science, the method that would allow scientists to make informed decisions about what counts as a scientific theory. The importance of demarcating good science from pseudo-science is neither otiose nor a mere philosophical exercise. It is at the very heart of science policy, when decisions are taken at the governmental level about how to spend taxpayers' money.

Karl Popper was, undoubtedly, one of the most influential philosophers of the early twentieth century to have contributed to the debate about demarcating good science from pseudo-science. In this section we very briefly review some of his seminal ideas, especially since such ideas will prove important for understanding methodological discussions about cosmology in the next two chapters.

Popper's battleground was the social sciences (Ladyman 2002; Thornton 2013). At the beginning of the twentieth century, in the German-speaking world, a lively debate took place between the so-called *Naturwissenschaften* (the natural sciences, including mathematics, physics, and chemistry) and the

Geisteswissenschaften (the human sciences, including psychology and the emergent psychoanalysis), and whether the latter could rise to the status of proper sciences on a par with the natural sciences. This is the historical context in which Popper began his philosophical reflections in the 1920s. Popper's reflections were influenced by the Vienna Circle, a group of young intellectuals including Philipp Frank for physics, Hans Hahn for mathematics, Otto Neurath for economics, and the philosophers Moritz Schlick (who joined the group in 1922) and Rudolf Carnap (who joined in 1926). The philosophical view adopted by the Vienna Circle is known as logical empiricism: knowledge comes in two kinds; the first kind is knowledge of logical truths (truths independent of experience); the second is empirical knowledge, whose truths are based on experience (see Gillies 1993). Popper's influential book *The Logic of Scientific Discovery* was first published in 1934 (the English translation came much later, in 1959) in the Vienna Circle series edited by Schlick; and it dealt precisely with the problem of how to demarcate good science from pseudo-science. Before Popper, the received view about scientific knowledge and the method of science was **inductivism**: on this view, scientific theories are confirmed by inductive inferences from an increasing number of positive instances to a universally valid conclusion. For example, Newton's second law seems confirmed by many positive instances from the pendulum, to harmonic oscillators and free fall, among others. We can think of scientific theories as sets of sentences, i.e. laws of nature; and laws of nature, as taking the form of true universal generalizations, 'For all objects x, if Fx then Gx' (e.g. Newton's second law would read as follows: if an external force acts on a body of mass m, then the body will accelerate). And we can think of true universal generalizations as being confirmed when a sufficiently large number of positive instances (and no negative instances) have been found for them. Inductivism was at work in the logical empiricists' criterion of **verification**: namely the idea that any claim or statement is scientific if there is a way of *empirically verifying* it (i.e. if there is a way of finding positive empirical instances confirming that claim or statement).

The problem with inductive methodology – according to Popper – is that it is too liberal as a method for demarcating good science from pseudo-science. Political theories such as Marxism or Freud's psychoanalysis would equally meet the requirements of inductivism. A Freudian psychoanalyst could appeal to plenty of positive instances of people's dreams that can confirm the validity of Freud's analysis of the Oedipus complex, for example. But is this per se sufficient to license the scientific status of Freud's psychoanalysis? People that read horoscopes can similarly claim that there are positive instances in their monthly working schedule confirming the horoscope's warning that it is going to be a very demanding month for Aquarians! Does it mean that horoscopes are scientific? Positive instances are where one wants to find them. Thus, to demarcate good science from pseudo-science, Popper thought, we need to probe a little deeper.

The problem – as Popper saw it – is that theories such as psychoanalysis do not make specific predictions, and their general principles are so broadly construed as to be compatible with any particular observations, whereas scientific theories such as Copernicus' heliocentric theory or Einstein's relativity do make novel predictions, i.e. predictions of new phenomena or entities. As the historian Koyré once said, the amazing thing about Copernican astronomy is that it worked, despite the overcast sky of Copernicus' Poland! Using Copernican astronomy, Galileo could predict the phases of Venus, a novel phenomenon not predicted by Ptolemaic astronomy and observed by Galileo himself with his telescope. Or consider Einstein's general relativity, which predicted light-bending, a phenomenon indeed observed by Arthur Eddington's expedition to Brazil in 1919. What makes Copernicus' or Einstein's theory 'scientific' is not just having positive instances, but instead, being able to make very specific and precise predictions about previously undreamt-of phenomena – predictions that *may turn out to be wrong*.

Popper's conclusion was that scientists should be looking for instances that are risky predictions, namely **potential falsifiers** (predictions that if proved wrong, would reject the theory). Having no potential falsifiers is the hallmark of dubious scientific standing. Pseudo-scientific theories have a tendency to *accommodate* evidence, as opposed to *predicting* novel, risky phenomena. But no matter how many positive instances of a generalization one has observed or accommodated, there is still no guarantee that the next instance will not falsify it. No matter how many white swans we might have observed, nothing excludes the possibility that the next observed swan will be black, as indeed explorers found in Australia. Hence, Popper's conclusion that the distinctive method of science does not consist in confirming hypotheses, but in falsifying them, looking for one crucial piece of negative evidence that may refute the whole theory.

According to Popper, science proceeds by a method of **conjectures and refutations**: scientists start with bold (theoretically and experimentally unwarranted) conjectures about some phenomena, deduce novel undreamt-of predictions, and then go about finding potential falsifiers for those predictions. Currently accepted scientific theories have passed severe tests and have survived, without being falsified as yet. If a theory does not pass severe tests, and/or if there are no sufficient or suitable potential falsifiers for it, the theory cannot be said to be scientific. The history of science is full of theories that enjoyed a relative period of empirical success until they were eventually falsified and rejected: from the caloric theory of Lavoisier (which regarded heat as an imponderable fluid) to Stahl's phlogiston theory in the eighteenth century, and Newton's ether theory. Science has grown across centuries by dismantling and rejecting previously successful theories – scientific progress is characterized and made possible by falsification.

To conclude, falsificationism is the distinctive method of science, according to Popper. It is a deductive (instead of inductive) method, whereby scientists start with bold conjectures, and deduce novel predictions, which then they go about testing. If the predictions prove wrong, the conjecture is falsified and replaced with a new one. If the predictions prove correct, the conjecture is corroborated and will continue to be employed to make further predictions and pass more tests, until proven wrong. However, reality is much more complex than Popper's simple deductive scheme. In daily laboratory situations, scientists never test a scientific hypothesis or conjecture by itself. Nor can they deduce any empirical consequence out of any bold conjecture either. This problem, known as the Duhem–Quine thesis, is the topic of our next section.

The Duhem–Quine thesis: or, the problem of underdetermination of theory by evidence

Before Popper developed falsificationism as the method of science, the French physicist Pierre Duhem (1906/1991) at the turn of the century had already realized that no scientific hypothesis can be tested in isolation, but only in conjunction with other main theoretical hypotheses plus some auxiliary ones. Consider Newton's law of gravity. Scientists never test the hypothesis of gravitation by itself, but always in conjunction with other theoretical hypotheses H_1, H_2, H_3 (e.g. Newton's three laws of motion) plus some auxiliary hypotheses A_1, A_2, A_3 (e.g. A_1 says that the mass of the sun is much bigger than the mass of other planets; A_2 says that no other force apart from the gravitational one is acting on the planets; A_3 says that planetary attractions are weaker than attractions between the sun and the planets). Now, suppose we deduce from this set of main and auxiliary hypotheses some observable evidence e and we proceed to test whether e occurs or not in nature:

$$H \& H_1 \& H_2 \& H_3 \& A_1 \& A_2 \& A_3 \rightarrow \text{evidence } e$$

Suppose we find that e does not occur (or that the measured value for e is not what one would expect from this set of hypotheses). This would only indicate that there must be something wrong with the whole set of hypotheses:

$$H \& H_1 \& H_2 \& H_3 \& A_1 \& A_2 \& A_3 \rightarrow \text{evidence } e$$
Not e

Then not-($H \& H_1 \& H_2 \& H_3 \& A_1 \& A_2 \& A_3$)

But we do not know whether it is H or H_1 or H_2 or H_3 or A_1 or A_2 or A_3, or any combination of any of these main and auxiliary hypotheses, which is actually refuted by the negative evidence. Duhem concluded that confirmation is not a process exhausted by comparing a single hypothesis with some observational evidence. The same (or very similar) observational evidence can in fact be entailed by more than one theory (and sometimes even incompatible theories) so that evidence may underdetermine the choice between theories: evidence may not provide us with strong reasons for accepting one theory over rival ones (obtained by tweaking one or more of either main or auxiliary hypotheses). This is what philosophers of science (see Stanford 2013) call the problem of **underdetermination of theory by evidence**.

The American philosopher W. V. O. Quine in a famous (1951) article further developed Duhem's idea. Quine arrived at a conclusion similar to Duhem's by criticizing what he considered as two dogmas of logical empiricism, namely **reductionism** and the **synthetic/analytic distinction**. Carnap's physicalism is a good example of reductionism: it claimed to reduce the whole system of science to the language of physics so as to guarantee intersubjective agreement. Quine argued that the logical empiricist's criterion of verification underpinned the reductionist claim that any theoretical statement can be reduced to an observational statement (i.e. a statement cashed out in a language that eschewed theoretical terms, e.g. 'electron', and used only terms referring to phenomena that could be easily observed and empirically verified). It underpinned also the analytic/synthetic distinction, since analytic statements are not amenable to being empirically verified, by contrast with synthetic statements. Since any attempt to define analyticity failed, and the analytic/synthetic distinction does not really stand, Quine concluded that we should dismiss the logical empiricist's criterion of verification, and replace it with a holistic approach, whereby we take each statement as related to the entire web of our knowledge. In Quine's words (1951, pp. 42–3):

> The totality of our so-called knowledge or beliefs, from the most casual matters of geography and history to the profoundest laws of atomic physics or even of pure mathematics and logic, is a man-made fabric, which impinges on experience only along the edges. A conflict with experience at the periphery occasions readjustments in the interior of the field … but the total field is so underdetermined by its boundary conditions, experience, that there is much latitude of choice as to what statements to re-evaluate in the light of any single contrary experience. No particular experiences are linked with any particular statements in the interior of the field, except indirectly through considerations of equilibrium affecting the field as a whole.

Given this holistic picture, the process of confirmation or refutation of a hypothesis can no longer be regarded as a one-to-one comparison between the hypothesis and a piece of evidence. Instead, it takes place through a variety of direct and indirect routes across the entire web of knowledge. Of course, Quine claimed, there are peripheral areas of the web (say biology) that are more directly exposed to experience, and hence more suitable to being confronted with it directly. There are, on the contrary, internal areas, such as logic or mathematics, which are less exposed to direct empirical evidence. But this does not mean that those areas (logic or mathematics) are analytic, i.e. that their truths are not grounded on matters of fact, or that they cannot be refuted by experience. By contrast with logical empiricism, Quine believed that even the most fundamental principles of mathematics are amenable to being refuted by experience. The extent to which different statements are subject to the 'tribunal of experience' depends on how far they are from the edges of the web, and how entrenched they are in it. Thus, suppose again we get a piece of negative evidence. How can we know which element of the web, which particular belief, this negative piece of evidence is going to refute? If there is leeway in the way evidence relates to any particular belief in the web, how do we know what to change in the web itself? This has become known as the Duhem–Quine thesis, namely how theory choice may be underdetermined by evidence, a topic that we will go back to in Chapter 3 in the context of our discussion about theory choice in contemporary cosmology. But we want to finish this chapter by introducing another philosopher of science, whose reflections on scientific knowledge and the method of science have been hugely influential over the past half century: Thomas Kuhn.

Thomas Kuhn's *Structure of Scientific Revolutions*

In the 1950s, the Duhem–Quine thesis brought to the general attention the problem of how in science the available evidence may not be sufficient to determine theory choice one way or another. While Popper's falsificationism had celebrated the role of evidence and severe experimental tests as the benchmark for good science, the Duhem–Quine thesis showed the limits of experimental evidence and the impossibility of the very idea of a 'crucial experiment', able to establish one way or another the fortunes of any theory. It is against this backdrop that in a seminal book published in 1962, entitled *The Structure of Scientific Revolutions*, the US philosopher of science Thomas Kuhn offered a highly influential, radically new conception of how science grows and unfolds.

Both the logical empiricists and Popper had thought of scientific knowledge as a largely incremental affair. As scientific inquiry proceeds, and new evidence is found, our scientific knowledge accumulates (by either inductively confirming or deductively falsifying theoretical hypotheses). In this way – the pre-Kuhn received view argued – we gradually acquire better and better scientific knowledge. Scientific progress would be secured by the right scientific method, which would deliver theories more and more likely to be true.

But this irenic picture of how science grows and unfolds clashed with the lessons coming from the history of science. Kuhn began his career in physics and during a postdoctoral position at Harvard, had the chance to study and teach a course in the history of science dedicated to Aristotelian physics. The difficulty encountered in making sense of outmoded lines of reasoning had a profound influence in the way Kuhn came to rethink scientific inquiry as a non-cumulative process of knowledge acquisition, with no distinctive (inductive or deductive) method. Most importantly, it reshaped radically Kuhn's view of scientific progress by rescinding the link between progress and **truth**, understood as the ability of a theory to capture things correctly. Instead, for Kuhn, science is characterized by three-stage cycles of **normal science, crises,** and **scientific revolutions**. During normal science, a scientific community works on a well-defined **scientific paradigm.** Although Kuhn never defined exactly the notion of 'scientific paradigm', he thought a scientific paradigm (or what he later called a 'disciplinary matrix') would typically include the dominant scientific theory, the experimental and technological resources, no less than the system of values of the community at a given time (e.g. how the community may value judgements of simplicity, accuracy, plausibility, and so on). In addition, a scientific paradigm includes also what Kuhn called 'exemplars', i.e. 'the concrete problem-solutions that students encounter from the start of their scientific education, whether in laboratories, on examinations, or at the ends of chapters in science texts' (1962/1996, Postscript, p. 187). Any scientific community in periods of normal science acquires its identity by working on an accepted textbook (be it Ptolemy's *Almagest*, or Newton's *Principia*) and solving well-defined problems or puzzles within a well-defined textbook tradition. No attempt to test, falsify, or refute the accepted paradigm takes place during periods of normal science.

Only when a sufficiently large number of anomalies – which cannot be done away with – accumulate, does the accepted paradigm undergo a period of crisis. In periods of crises, a new paradigm may come to the fore, and the crisis resolves into a scientific revolution when the scientific community decides to abandon the old paradigm and shift consensus around the new paradigm. Kuhn stressed how theory choice in these cases is not determined by the alleged superiority of the new paradigm over the old one. The consensus-gathering process is not determined by the new paradigm being more likely to be true or correct than the old one, but by the increase in the puzzle-solving power of the new paradigm. The new paradigm should be able to solve more puzzles than the old one, and thus Kuhn redefined scientific progress in terms of increased puzzle-solving. But this shift of focus from Popper's falsification to Kuhn's puzzle-solving has far-reaching implications for the rationality of theory choice.

Kuhn famously claimed that scientific paradigms (say, Ptolemaic astronomy and Copernican astronomy) are incommensurable. **Incommensurability** meant lack of a 'common measure' to evaluate two paradigms (not to be confused with non-comparability or non-communicability) – in other words, lack of a common measure for rational choice between paradigms. Different paradigms use different scientific concepts, methodologies, resources, and even systems of values, so that – Kuhn concluded – paradigm shifts resemble psychologists' *Gestalt switches* rather than rational, objective decision-making processes. Kuhn's (1962/1996, p. 121) radical conclusion was that 'although the world does not change with a change of paradigm, the scientist afterward works in a different world'. A lot could be said about incommensurability and its implications for our views about science, but we will have to leave those reflections for some other occasion (see Bird 2011). We will go back to incommensurability and the rationality of theory choice in Chapter 3, when we review the prospects of a possible paradigm shift in contemporary cosmology. (Is there any crisis looming for our currently accepted paradigm in cosmology?)

Chapter summary

- We began by exploring the difficulty of explaining exactly what constitutes genuine scientific endeavour, as opposed to non-scientific endeavours.
- We then discussed epistemic relativism as the view that denies the existence of universal norms of reasoning and standards for justifying knowledge claims, and its implications for realism as the view that says that scientific theories aim to deliver a true story about nature and that progress should be thought of in terms of getting closer to the truth. This debate is important for understanding the nature of scientific knowledge and whether there might be a distinctive method for scientific claims.
- Next we considered Karl Popper's famous solution to the problem of demarcating science from pseudo-science in terms of falsification. We clarified Popper's criticism of inductivism and his view of the scientific method as consisting of conjectures and refutations.
- Then we turned our attention to the Duhem–Quine thesis, which says that theory choice is underdetermined by the available evidence. We looked at both Duhem's and Quine's lines of reasoning behind the thesis.
- Finally, we considered how the problem of underdetermination of theory by evidence was further explored in a radically new way of thinking about science, due to Thomas Kuhn. On this proposal, scientific change that takes place when scientific revolutions occur is not to be thought of as an incremental, rational process from an old scientific theory to a new one. Instead, scientific change takes the form of a shift between two *incommensurable* scientific paradigms, and raises issues about the rationality of theory choice.
- Both Popper's falsificationism, underdetermination of theory by evidence and the rationality of theory choice will feature prominently in the next two chapters when we discuss the methodological problems and prospects of contemporary cosmology.

Study questions

1 What is epistemic relativism? What does it challenge?
2 Why are discussions about whether or not science has a distinctive method important?
3 In your own words, try to explain what it means for a scientific theory to be empirically testable.
4 What is the difference between a theory being empirically testable and it being empirically falsifiable?
5 What did Popper mean by 'potential falsifier'?
6 What does the Duhem–Quine thesis say?
7 Can you briefly explain in your own words, what Duhem's and Quine's respective contributions to the thesis are?

8 What is the problem of underdetermination of theory by evidence? What does it challenge?
9 Try to explain in your own words Kuhn's account of the structure of scientific revolutions. How did it change the received view of scientific progress?
10 What is a scientific paradigm, according to Kuhn?
11 What did Kuhn mean by paradigms being incommensurable? And how does incommensurability relate to the problem of underdetermination of theory by evidence?

Introductory further reading

Achinstein, P. (2010) 'Scientific knowledge', in S. Bernecker and D. H. Pritchard (eds) *Routledge Companion to Epistemology*, London: Routledge, chapter 32. (A fairly comprehensive introductory overview of the main issues regarding scientific knowledge.)

Boghossian, P. (2006) *Fear of Knowledge: Against Relativism and Constructivism*, Oxford: Oxford University Press.

Chalmers, A. F. (1999) *What Is This Thing Called Science?*, 3rd edn, Milton Keynes: Open University Press. (One of the most widely used contemporary introductions to philosophy of science, and for good reason, as it is a superb outline of the main issues in this area: accessible, authoritative, and very readable.)

Giere, R. (2006) *Scientific Perspectivism*, Chicago: University of Chicago Press. (A recent trend in the philosophy of science with wide-ranging implications for the debate about truth and relativism.)

Kuhn, T. S. (1962/1996) *The Structure of Scientific Revolutions*, 3rd edn, Chicago: University of Chicago Press. (A cult book that has shaped and changed the course of philosophy of science in the past half century.)

Ladyman, J. (2002) *Understanding Philosophy of Science*, London: Routledge. (One of the best introductory textbooks of the past two decades. Accessible, well-written, and informative.)

Popper, K. (1959) *The Logic of Scientific Discovery*, London: Routledge. (Another cult book in the philosophy of science. Must be read by anyone who wants to get acquainted with the field.)

Advanced further reading

Duhem, P. (1906/1991) *The Aim and Structure of Physical Theory*, Princeton: Princeton University Press. (This is the classic book, where the problem of underdetermination was first expounded.)

Gillies, D. (1993) *Philosophy of Science in the Twentieth Century*, Oxford: Blackwell. (An excellent, if intellectually demanding, account of contemporary themes in the philosophy of science. See especially the chapter on logical empiricism and Popper.)

Goldacre, B. (2009) *Bad Science*, London: Harper Collins. (We can't recommend this book highly enough. Although it is not a text on the philosophy of science, reading this book will give you a fantastic introduction to the scientific method and why it is so important.)

Kusch, M. (2002) *Knowledge by Agreement*, Oxford: Oxford University Press. (An excellent introduction, by a world-leading expert, to the epistemological view that says scientific knowledge is a social phenomenon, with important implications for the debate about relativism and realism.)

Quine, W. V. O. (1951) 'Two dogmas of empiricism', *Philosophical Review* 60: 20–43. (An all-time classic on the problem of underdetermination. It builds on Duhem's pioneering work and further develops the thesis. Very advanced reading.)

Rorty, R. (1979) *Philosophy and the Mirror of Nature*, Princeton: Princeton University Press. (An all-time classic text that has deeply influenced the debate about epistemic relativism.)

Siegel, H. (2011) 'Epistemological relativism: arguments pro and con', in S. Hales (ed.) *A Companion to Relativism*, Oxford: Blackwell, chapter 11.

Sosa, E. (1991) *Knowledge in Perspective*, Cambridge: Cambridge University Press.

Internet resources

Bird, A. (2011) 'Thomas Kuhn', in E. N. Zalta (ed.) *Stanford Encyclopedia of Philosophy* [online encyclopedia], http://plato.stanford.edu/entries/thomas-kuhn/ (An excellent summary of Kuhn's work in the philosophy of science, written by an expert in the field.)

Stanford, K. (2013) 'Underdetermination of scientific theory', in E. N. Zalta (ed.) *Stanford Encyclopedia of Philosophy* [online encyclopedia], http://plato.stanford.edu/entries/scientific-underdetermination/ (accessed 4 June 2014) (A very thorough and up-to-date exposition by a leading expert on this topic.)

Thornton, S. (2013) 'Karl Popper', in E. N. Zalta (ed.) *Stanford Encyclopedia of Philosophy* [online encyclopedia], http://plato.stanford.edu/entries/popper/ (accessed 4 June 2014) (A comprehensive introduction to the philosophy of Popper.)

2 The origins of our universe

Laws, testability and observability in cosmology

Michela Massimi and John Peacock

Introduction: cosmology – from a branch of metaphysics to scientific discipline

Over the past few years, philosophers of science have paid increasing attention to cosmology. This renewed philosophical attention to cosmology comes in the aftermath of the experimental confirmation of an accelerating expansion of the universe (via observations of Type Ia supernovae, for which the 2011 Nobel Prize was awarded). It comes also at a time when cosmology is witnessing a wealth of new data coming from large spectroscopic and photometric galaxy surveys, designed to give an answer to pressing questions about the existence of **dark matter** and **dark energy**.

For a very long time, cosmology was regarded as somehow having a special status compared with other sciences, closer to philosophy than to mathematical physics. Although the study of the cosmos was well known to ancient civilizations (from the Babylonians to ancient Greeks and the Maya, among others), the term 'cosmology' is much more recent (dating back to the seventeenth or eighteenth century). And even then, the term was often used interchangeably with 'cosmogony', as a generic term for any theory about the origin of the universe. Such cosmogonies were often of philosophical-religious flavour, and involved speculations that eluded the mathematical rigour and experimental tests typical of the new sciences emerging with the scientific revolution.

Consider Newton's *Mathematical Principles of Natural Philosophy* (1st edn, 1687). This extraordinary book laid the foundations of modern physics, by providing testable laws of nature that could explain a variety of observed phenomena (from free fall to planetary motions). Yet Newton's mathematical physics did not explain what set planets in motion at the origins of the universe. Explaining the origins of our universe, how planets and stars formed, how they evolved, and what set them in motion, was beyond the scope of Newton's *Principia*. And the task was often taken up by philosophers in the context of either a discussion of Newton's natural philosophy (e.g. Maupertuis in his 1732 *Discours sur les différentes figures des astres*), or in the context of metaphysics. For example, the German philosopher Alexander Baumgarten (1714–62) in his 1739 book *Metaphysics*, Part 2 (§§351–2) dedicated to Cosmology, distinguished between *empirical cosmology* as the 'science based upon experience that is nearest to hand', and *rational cosmology* 'based upon the concept of the world'. He concluded that since cosmology contained the first principles of psychology, physics, theology, teleology, and practical philosophy, cosmology should belong to metaphysics. A similar classification of cosmology can also be found in another influential German philosopher of the time, Christian Wolff (1679–1754) in his *Cosmologia generalis*. Why was cosmology regarded as a branch of metaphysics? And why did it take so long for cosmology to become a science in its own right? An easy answer to both questions comes to the fore. One may be tempted to reply that cosmology could not have risen to the status of a proper science until sufficient technological advances made available the right kind of data. Yet, this answer – simple and natural as it is – is not sufficient to answer these questions. A more comprehensive answer to these questions has to address the relation between cosmology and metaphysics in the eighteenth century, first; and, second, the specific problems and challenges that cosmology faces as a science. Let us discuss each of these two points in turn.

That cosmology was for so long regarded as a branch of metaphysics should not come as a surprise. While Newton in the *Principia* offered rigorous mathematical demonstrations of phenomena and refused to indulge in speculative hypotheses about the *causes* of those phenomena, the job of speculating about the *causes* of phenomena (and, the very first causes of the world) was left to theologians and metaphysicians. Thus, cosmology, in works such as those of Baumgarten or Wolff, became a rational exercise in examining the concept of the 'world' or 'universe' as a multitude of finite beings; the nature of their interconnections; the contingency and necessity of the parts and the whole – and so forth. In the aftermath of *Principia*, across the Continent (in Germany in particular) there was a widespread feeling that Newton's mathematical method was insufficient to shed light on key questions about the origins of the universe. This widespread feeling, and the necessity of supplementing Newton's mathematical demonstrations with metaphysical foundations, found its most influential expression in the work of the German philosopher Immanuel Kant (1724–1804). One of the first attempts at a modern metaphysical explanation of the origin of the universe, according to Newtonian principles, can be found in Kant's 1755 *Universal Natural History and Theory of the Heavens*, whose subtitle reads *Essay on the constitution and the mechanical origins of the whole universe according to Newtonian principles*. In this text, Kant hypothesized that the universe at its origin was not a vast empty space (as Newtonian physics suggested), but was instead filled with a 'fine matter', on which two fundamental, Newtonian forces acted. *Attraction* was a force capable of lumping the fine matter into what became the bodies of planets and stars; *repulsion* was a force balancing attraction and causing fine matter to whirl in vortices that would become the nucleation sites for planets and stars. While both attraction and repulsion can be found in Newton as fundamental forces of nature, both in the *Principia* and in the *Optics*, Kant's original take on Newton consisted in using these two forces to offer an explanation of the presumed mechanism at play in the constitution of the universe. Kant's explanation in terms of a counterbalance between attraction and repulsion of 'fine matter' diffused across space, provided metaphysical foundations for Newton's physics, foundations that at the time were regarded as essential for answering open cosmological questions. In so doing, Kant also laid the foundations of what became later known as the **Kant–Laplace nebular hypothesis**, one of the very first attempts at a scientific explanation of the origins of the universe from an original nebula of gases (see Brush 1996). Here we see exemplified a first important interaction between philosophy and the sciences. Kant's 1755 cosmogony shows how philosophy (in this case, metaphysics) played a heuristic role in the development of some important scientific ideas.

Yet Kant himself remained sceptical about the possibility of developing cosmology as a science, because the metaphysical idea of a universe having a beginning in time and space seemed fraught with contradictions (what Kant called **antinomies of reason** in his mature work). To Kant's eyes, metaphysics did not give a clear answer to the big questions about the origins and evolution of the universe. Thus, at the end of the eighteenth century the prospects of further developing cosmology as a branch of metaphysics looked dim, and the path to cosmology as a science seemed still very long. Why did it take so long for cosmology to become a science in its own right? It was not just that the eighteenth-century metaphysical foundations of cosmology proved fraught with contradictions. Three main problems stood in the way of developing cosmology as a science in its own right. We review each of them briefly here.

1 Laws of nature

Scientific theories allow scientists to make inferences based on laws of nature. For example, given Newton's law of gravity, scientists can make inferences about planetary motions no less than the free fall of an apple, or the times of the tides. Philosophers of science have long been investigating what a law of nature is, and the allegedly universal validity and necessity of the laws. A specific problem arises in cosmology when we try to use our current laws of nature to make inferences about the origins of our universe. How can we be sure that the same laws of nature we know and love today, apply also to the origins of the universe? Did not our laws presumably come into existence with the existence of our universe? How can we extrapolate from the present physics and its laws to the physics of the early universe?

A similar sceptical line of reasoning prompted the physicist and philosopher Ernst Mach at the end of the nineteenth century to object to Newton's famous two-globe experiment as an argument for the existence of **absolute space**. Newton argued that in an imaginary empty universe with only two globes attached via a string and rotating relative to each other, we would observe the rope become tense because of acceleration acting on the two globes. And he postulated the existence of an infinite, boundless space (which he called absolute space) as the privileged frame of reference for the observed forces (since, after all, by definition there are no other material objects with respect to which the two globes may be accelerating in an empty universe). But against Newton, Mach retorted that speculating what might happen to our familiar intuitions about two globes attached to a string in an imaginary empty universe involves a huge 'inductive leap' (from daily situations to a hypothetical, not empirically verifiable scenario) and, hence an unwarranted extrapolation (see Sklar 1974, p. 186). The same line of reasoning would warn us against applying familiar physics to the early universe, and extrapolating from current laws of daily scenarios to the origins of our universe.

2 *Uniqueness*

The other problem with cosmology is the uniqueness of its object of investigation: our universe (for a discussion of this point, see Smeenk 2013, §4). If cosmology has to have the status of an experimental science, it should be possible to run experiments to test hypotheses. But running an experiment typically involves being able to repeat the test more than once, and on several different samples. For example, to test the law of free fall, Galileo had to perform the same experiment with balls rolling down planes of different lengths and inclinations. Or, when in the nineteenth century, the physicists Fizeau, Foucault and Maxwell performed tests to establish the value of the velocity of light in empty space, they repeated the same experiment with a beam of light going through spinning mirrors across a variety of media (water, air). If repeating tests on *multiple samples* of the same kind (e.g. Galileo's inclined planes) and/or in *different circumstances* (e.g. in air or water) is key to testing a scientific theory, then again the prospects for cosmology as a science may look prima facie unpromising. We have only one universe to observe and experiment upon – ours. In the words of a prominent physicist (Ellis 2014, p. 6): 'Cosmology is the unique case where there is no similar entity with which we can compare the object of study, because by definition the Universe is all that there is'. So, if *testability* so conceived is a distinctive feature of experimental science, cosmology seems to face a problem.

3 *Unobservability*

A third problem with cosmology, somehow related to the first one, concerns the extent to which we can extrapolate information from our current vantage point (our planet Earth) to the universe as a whole. The problem does not affect just theoretical inferences based on laws of nature, which might break down or not be valid at the origins of our universe. It affects also the amount of information and data we can access from our vantage point, considering the speed-of-light limit, which constrains how far back into the history of our universe we can 'observe', so to speak. There are bound to be vast regions of our universe that will remain unobservable from the vantage point of an observer on Earth.

The unobservability of scientific entities has been at the centre of a lively debate in philosophy of science over the past 30 years between defenders of so-called scientific realism, who claim that our beliefs in the existence of unobservable entities (be they electrons, quarks, DNA, bacteria or other) is justified, and defenders of a variety of scientific anti-realism (for details about this debate, see Massimi 2013). Let us be clear on this point. The unobservability affecting cosmology has nothing to do with its objects being not-observable-to-our-naked-eyes (as in the realism–anti-realism debate), although cosmologists often resort to computer techniques to produce visualizations of cosmological entities. Nor does unobservability affect scientists' ability to make theoretical inferences about the universe. Progress can be made by starting with educated guesses, such as the **cosmological principle**, that the universe is homogeneous and isotropic, i.e. it is the same in all spatial positions and directions, no matter from which vantage point it may be observed. Initially, we only know that conditions are isotropic from the vantage point of the Milky Way, so it is a significant leap to assert that this property must hold for all observers. To make such an argument, it is necessary to add the **Copernican principle**: that our place in the universe should not be special. Although this sounds like common sense, it is clearly a critical extra step. But having made this assumption, we gain the framework of a simple uniform universe to act as a model for the interpretation of data. Better still, with sufficient data, the initial guess can be tested: we now possess three-dimensional surveys of the positions of around 1 million galaxies, from which it is possible to verify that the density of galaxies is indeed highly uniform on sufficiently large scales – i.e. the cosmological principle has moved from being an educated guess to something that is supported empirically.

This need for cosmology to proceed in such an initially ill-founded manner highlights a specific problem about unobservability in cosmology: our vantage point as observers in the universe constrains *all the information we can access* to the events in the so-called **past light cone**, i.e. parts of space that have been able to send information to us. This **horizon problem** comes in two forms with different degrees of severity. At the most basic level, objects more than about a distance ct away (where c is the speed of light) cannot be seen before a time t; this in itself is not a huge objection in principle, since it might be presumed that our horizon will grow and any object will eventually be seen, however distant. But in an accelerating universe, there exists an **event horizon**: points sufficiently far apart can never contact each other.

Despite these three distinctive methodological problems, cosmology has come a long way from the time of the Kant–Laplace nebular hypothesis, and has established itself as a scientific discipline in its own right within just over a century. The path that led cosmology from a branch of metaphysics to a proper science has not been without difficulties and lively philosophical discussions. Still in 1950, W. H. McCrea complained that cosmology was a 'highly unsatisfactory subject', and in 1954, G. J. Whitrow (1954, p. 272) lamented that 'many physicists find it [i.e. cosmology] so baffling compared to other branches of physics that they pay as little attention to current cosmological theories as to the original theory of Thales'. In the next section, we briefly review some of the milestones in the history of theoretical and observational cosmology of the last century. We return to the issues of laws, uniqueness and unobservability at the end of the chapter, where we draw some philosophical conclusions about what philosophers can learn from the practice of cosmology.

The expanding universe: a very brief history of observational and theoretical cosmology

The history of cosmology shows a striking interplay of empirical discovery integrated into a theoretically motivated framework. The pace of this progress has been astonishingly rapid: a century ago, our general knowledge about the important features of the universe barely differed from that of the stone age, whereas today there is a sense that observational study of the universe is converging. This may seem paradoxical: how can our knowledge of a (probably infinite) universe be complete? The answer is that we inhabit an evolving universe, which we study using signals that propagate at the speed of light. This latter fact is convenient in that it leads to the cliché that 'telescopes are time machines' – we see distant parts of the universe as they were in the deep past. But at early enough times, rather little had happened; in particular the galaxies that host the stars and planets important for life had yet to form. In some areas of the sky, we have thus been able to use instruments like the Hubble Space Telescope to look back to a time before the galaxies existed – so we know that no more than about 100 billion galaxies exist to be imaged even if we could study the whole sky with unlimited sensitivity. Within a decade, it is possible that a significant fraction of this task will have been accomplished. But it is not necessary to go so far, as we already know that the universe is highly uniform on large scales, so progress in understanding the history of the expanding universe is possible by studying only part of it. The fraction that has been observed in detail is now large enough that future observations will only shrink statistical errors that are already rather small in most cases.

The discovery of the expanding universe makes an interesting piece of history. As is often the case in science, cosmology has its 'creation myth' in the form of a simplified story that is seriously at variance with the actual events. It is thus 'well known' that the expansion of the universe was discovered by Edwin Hubble in 1929, when he demonstrated that galaxies displayed a **redshift** (displacement of spectral features to longer wavelengths) that increased linearly with distance. Assuming for the present that the redshift can be interpreted as a Doppler shift indicating a radial velocity, v, this result can be written as Hubble's law relating the velocity to distance, D: $v = HD$ (the issue of how to interpret the redshift is discussed in detail below). The constant of proportionality is the **Hubble constant**; this is now known to be about 70 km s^{-1} Mpc^{-1} (1 Mpc is 3×10^{22} m, which is also the typical distance between galaxies). The reciprocal of H has the unit of time, with a value of about 14 billion years; as we will see, this tells us that the expansion of the universe has been taking place for about such a period. This can be made plausible by considering the simplest model for Hubble's law: a single explosion. Explode a grenade at a point at time $t = 0$ and debris will fly off at various speeds, reaching distances $D = v \, t$. Thus, we get Hubble's law with $H = 1/t$. This is a dangerous analogy with the true **Big Bang**, which was absolutely not a single explosion that filled previously empty space; nevertheless, it gives some insight into what Hubble's law might mean.

Perhaps the biggest problem with this tale is that the universal redshift, indicating expansion, was actually discovered by V. M. Slipher, at the Lowell Observatory in Arizona. For nearly a decade, starting in 1912, this virtuoso experimentalist was the only astronomer capable of making these observations, and the recent centenary of his revolutionary discovery received surprisingly little notice (although see Way and Hunter 2013). By 1917, Slipher had measured radial velocities for 25 galaxies, which were positive in twenty-one cases (four nearby galaxies actually approach the Milky Way). Thus the tendency for the system of galaxies to expand on average was already empirically demonstrated at this time. Establishing that the expansion is uniform (i.e. Hubble's law) is much harder – and we now know that Hubble's 1929 sample is far too shallow to prove such a relation convincingly.

But in the meantime, theorists had not been standing idle. Einstein wrote down his relativistic gravitational field equations in 1915, improving on Newton's law of gravity, which had survived unchanged for over two centuries. However, Einstein realized that his new equations did not solve a challenge that had puzzled Newton: what happens to an infinite uniform distribution of matter? Both Einstein and Newton thought that it was obvious that the matter should stay in place, based on the apparently unchanging nature of the heavens. But Einstein realized that this was only possible if there was some means of countering the gravitational force that would otherwise tend to pull the matter together. He therefore changed his field equations in 1917 specifically in order to permit a static cosmological solution – ironically unaware that Slipher's work had just rendered this unnecessary. Einstein's adjustment was to introduce the **cosmological constant**, Λ, which he viewed as representing the curvature of spacetime even in the absence of matter. Today, it is more common to view this as an energy density associated with the vacuum, so that all of space is in effect filled with a substance that cannot be removed (for which the modern name is dark energy – see next chapter). In any case, the gravitational effect of this term (discussed in more detail in the next chapter) opposes the attraction of normal matter, allowing the desired static universe. But almost immediately the situation became more complicated. In 1917, de Sitter showed that Einstein's field equations could be solved by a model that was completely empty apart from the cosmological constant – i.e. a model with no matter whatsoever, just dark energy. This was the first model of an expanding universe, although this was unclear at the time. The whole **principle of general relativity** was to write equations of physics that were valid for all observers, independently of the coordinates used. But this means that the same solution can be written in various different ways, some of which were easier to interpret than others. Thus de Sitter viewed his solution as static, but with a tendency for the rate of ticking of clocks to depend on position. This phenomenon was already familiar in the form of gravitational time dilation (clocks deep in gravitational potential wells run slow), so it is understandable that the de Sitter effect was viewed in the same way. It took a little while before it was proved (by Weyl, in 1923) that the prediction was of a redshifting of spectral lines that increased linearly with distance (i.e. Hubble's law). Now, experimental scientists love a theoretical prediction, as they can't lose by testing it; so it is unsurprising that a number of astronomers set out to search for the de Sitter effect as a tendency for redshift to increase with distance. And at least three of them had found such evidence prior to Hubble's 1929 paper. There is no doubt that Hubble was influenced by the de Sitter–Weyl prediction: he cites earlier searches, and concludes ' … the velocity-distance relation may represent the de Sitter effect … '. So this is far from being a pure observational discovery, unlike Slipher's pioneering efforts.

From an interpretative point of view, what is fascinating is that Hubble did not say 'the universe is expanding', and indeed it took some while for this to become clear. The general solution of Einstein's equations for matter plus cosmological constant was given in a pair of papers by the Soviet cosmologist Friedmann in 1922 and 1924. The second paper was especially notable for introducing the idea of an infinite open universe of negative spatial curvature. The idea of spatial curvature is already radical, but it can just about be grasped intuitively by considering the surface of a sphere as an example of a curved surface embedded in a three-dimensional space. By analogy, we might imagine that 3D space itself could share a similar property: unbounded, but finite, so that you return to your starting point if you attempt to travel along a straight line in a single direction. Such a model would be termed a **closed universe**, and Einstein thought it was very likely that the real universe should be closed in this way. But the mathematics of such curvature admits another possibility: negative curvature. This is actually impossible to visualize in the same way: the surface of a sphere has uniform positive curvature, but no surface of uniform negative curvature exists. The best that can be done is to think locally. Without spatial curvature, the angles of a triangle add up to 180 degrees, but a triangle drawn on a sphere will have angles summing to more than 180 degrees; the sign of negative curvature is that the sum would be less than 180 degrees. A saddle has a point of negative curvature where the rider sits. Realizing that the universe might have such a property – curved but still infinite – was a huge leap forward. But although Friedmann did say explicitly that his solutions were non-stationary, and that the curvature of space depended on time, a clear and direct statement that the universe was expanding, with galaxies moving apart from each other, was not given until Lemaître's 1927 work, and not really widely appreciated until this appeared in English translation in 1931.

But how certain are we that this modern way of looking at things is the correct, or indeed the only, way of interpreting the data? Empirically, answering this question is not so straightforward: we measure redshifted radiation here today, but we have no direct means of measuring the properties of the radiation as it was emitted, or of studying what happens to it en route. We know from terrestrial experiments that the frequency of radiation can be shifted either by the Doppler effect of motion, or gravitationally, so it is natural to assume that the cosmological effect is some combination of these effects. It is easy to show that gravitational time dilation should scale quadratically with distance, so that the Doppler effect should be the dominant process at small separations. It is striking that Slipher had the confidence to assert this interpretation in his first (1913) paper on galaxy spectroscopy ' ... we have at the present no other interpretation for it. Hence we may conclude that the Andromeda Nebula is approaching the solar system ... '. Although the velocity of Andromeda seems very small today (300 km s^{-1}), it was very large for the day, and its Doppler origin might have been queried.

Indeed, it is a reasonable concern that there might be physical mechanisms for frequency shifts that are only detectable on cosmological scales. A well-known example is Zwicky's 1929 **tired light** hypothesis: that photons lose energy as they travel over large distances through some unspecified dissipative effect. This can be tested in a number of ways, most simply using the fact that the Doppler shift is a form of time dilation: receding clocks appear to run more slowly. Atomic clocks are one example, leading to the shift of spectral lines, but the time dilation would also apply to macroscopic objects. A perfect example for this application is provided by Type Ia supernovae; these exploding stars are very nearly standard objects, both in their energy output and in the history of their emission, which rises to a peak about two weeks after explosion, and then declines over a similar period. These have been seen at large enough distances that the redshifting stretches wavelengths by over a factor of 3 – and indeed these distant supernovae appear to evolve more slowly by just this factor.

A more subtle alternative interpretation of redshifting is given by the concept of **expanding space**, which is a frequent source of confusion. The expansion of an ideal symmetric universe is uniform, so that the separations of all pairs of particles increase by a common factor over a given period of time. If the volume of the universe is finite, then the total volume of space undoubtedly increases with time – as can be seen intuitively in the common analogy of galaxies as dots painted on the surface of an inflating balloon. Moreover, the redshift factor turns out to be exactly proportional to the expansion factor: if we receive light from a galaxy where the wavelength of a spectral feature is twice the laboratory value, we know that this light was emitted when the universe was half its present size. This suggests a picture where the galaxies are not really moving, but the space between them is 'swelling up', stretching light as it does so; this explanation is to be found in innumerable introductory textbooks and semipopular articles. So what causes redshift? Is it the Doppler effect or expanding space? Or, are they equivalent descriptions of the same thing? At the level of a uniform universe, the expanding-space viewpoint may be more attractive, since it can deal simply with very large redshift factors, which require one to worry about relativistic corrections in a Doppler interpretation. But expanding space as a general concept is problematic, and can easily lead the unwary to incorrect conclusions. For example, does the expansion of space apply in the solar system? Is the Earth trying to move away from the sun? What prevents it from doing so?

The answer is that the expansion of space cannot be detected locally. The problem is that our physical intuition is influenced by imperfect analogies like the inflated balloon, where the rubber surface has friction. If you stood on a rubber sheet, you would notice if it stretched, since friction at your shoes would pull your feet apart – but what about a perfectly frictionless surface, such as an ice rink? There, the expanding surface would slide under your feet in an undetectable way. Similarly, there is no additional frictional force in three dimensions that corresponds to the expansion of the universe trying to pull things apart, even though it is unfortunately commonly believed to be the case. The issue here is related to the concept of the ether, which was the hypothetical medium whose oscillations constituted light waves. Prior to special relativity, there seemed to be a paradox: the speed of light should apparently depend on the motion of the observer relative to the ether, but no such effect had been detected. Einstein did not disprove the existence of the ether, but he explained why motions relative to it could not be detected. But a physical concept that cannot be detected is not of much practical use. A similar view should be taken of expanding space: it adds nothing to the simple view of the expanding universe as consisting locally of galaxy motions in a spacetime that is extremely close to that of special relativity.

Even once the basic nature of expansion at a given instant has been clearly grasped, however, the expanding universe has more puzzles in store once we think about its evolution. Running a video of the expansion backwards inevitably tells us that at earlier times the universe was denser and hotter. A little more thought along these lines shows that the energy density of the early universe was actually dominated by radiation, rather than ordinary matter. As things are compressed, conserving particles causes the density to rise: when the universe was half its present size, the volume was $2^3 = 8$ times smaller, so the number density of all particles was 8 times greater, including photons. But because of redshifting, each photon was twice as energetic in the past: so the energy density in radiation was 16 times greater. Continuing this process, and using $E = mc^2$, we can therefore see that the mass density of the universe will be dominated by the radiation if we go back far enough. And according to Einstein's relativistic theory of gravity, a radiation-dominated universe cannot expand forever: at a finite time in the past, the extrapolation of the expansion reaches a singularity, where the density becomes infinite.

This was recognized early on as a major problem, since, as we mentioned at the beginning of this chapter, the laws of physics cannot follow nature's behaviour to times before the singularity, on pain of a huge inductive leap. Fred Hoyle proposed instead the **steady-state universe**, in which matter was continually created so as to allow eternal expansion (i.e. the density was not larger in the past). In 1949, Hoyle criticized the simple radiation-dominated model as having an unexplained start as 'a big bang' – but there is now abundant evidence that the universe did pass through a hot and dense early phase, and the Big Bang is a commonly used term for this period.

The most direct evidence for a hot early phase is the **cosmic microwave background** (CMB, see Figure 2.1). This was discovered serendipitously in 1965, although its existence was predicted. It is inevitable that the universe must contain a **last scattering surface**, at the point where the temperature drops to a few thousand degrees and matter changes from an ionized plasma into neutral atoms. Thereafter, radiation can propagate freely, so that we should see the entire sky blazing like the surface of the sun – except cooled by the fact that the last scattering surface lies at high redshift. In practice, the observed radiation corresponds to a present-day temperature of 2.725 degrees (Kelvin), for which black-body emission peaks near a wavelength of 1 milli-metre; this originates when the universe was about 1,100 times smaller

Figure 2.1 An all-sky image of the cosmic microwave background, from the European Space Agency's Planck satellite. The emission at wavelengths around one millimetre has been carefully cleaned of contributions from our own Milky Way, to show the relic radiation that has been travelling since the universe was smaller than at present by a factor 1,100. The intensity displays small fluctuations of around 1 part in 100,000: these are the seeds of subsequent structure formation, and a window into the earliest times. According to the theory of inflationary cosmology, we are staring at amplified quantum fluc-tuations, generated when the entire visible universe was of subnuclear dimensions. (Copyright photo: European Space Agency)

than today. This is the furthest back in time we can ever see (about 400,000 years after the Big Bang singularity) using electromagnetic radiation, and it shows us the universe in a relatively simple state, prior to the formation of complex structures such as galaxies. The CMB is thus a treasure trove of information about the nature of the universe, and how it reached its present form.

In particular, the CMB radiation is found to contain small fluctuations with direction on the sky, of around 1 part in 100,000. These represent small fluctuations in the density of matter at early times, which are expected to grow under their own gravitational attraction into larger fluctuations today: the galaxies themselves, together with their large-scale clustering into super-clusters, which make up patterns of extent over 100 million light years. The existence of galaxy clustering has been known since the 1930s, and it was used to predict the necessity for small fluctuations in the CMB radiation, which were finally detected by NASA's *COBE* satellite in 1992. Observing the build-up of structure in the universe has been a great triumph, but it introduces another puzzle with the Big Bang: the way that gravitational instability works implies that the fluctuations in the curvature of spacetime remain constant at early times, so that the spacetime could not have been perfectly uniform near the time of the Big Bang. So not only did the entire expanding universe appear from nowhere, but it already carried within it the seeds of the future structure. All these strange initial conditions cry out for a direct explanation, which arose in the 1980s in the form of **inflationary cosmology**, discussed in Chapter 4.

But despite the puzzles associated with the Big Bang singularity, we can be confident that the Big Bang model does describe the universe for a large portion of its expansion. This conclusion does not require us to see directly beyond the last-scattering era, since there are indirect **relics** of earlier and hotter phases. The most well-understood of these relics is in the form of the light chemical elements. Via spectroscopy, we know that all stars are mostly composed of hydrogen, followed by helium (about 25 per cent of their mass), and trace amounts of all other elements. Although nuclear reactions in stars do generate helium, the lack of any hydrogen-only stars shows that the helium must have predated the first stars – i.e. it was formed by nuclear reactions at early times. The theory of **primordial nucleosynthesis** follows these reactions, and shows that the observed helium fraction is inevitable. This is a great triumph, giving an indirect view of conditions in the universe back to temperatures of around 10^{10} degrees (Kelvin) and times of 1 second.

Cosmology and scientific methodology: a primer

As we have seen, cosmology has successfully established itself as a science in its own right, in just over a century. As often in science, the success story of cosmology is entangled with theoretical predictions (from Hubble's law, to de Sitter's model, among others) no less than experimental discoveries (from the

CMB to the supernova Ia). What can philosophers learn from the history of cosmology? How does a branch of metaphysics become ultimately a scientific theory? In what follows, we go back to the three problems we identified at the beginning of this chapter (i.e. laws of nature, uniqueness, and unobservability) and place them within the wider context of philosophical and methodological discussions.

Laws of nature, perfect cosmological principle and cosmological natural selection

The first methodological problem that we mentioned at the beginning of this chapter was the difficulty in extrapolating the validity of our current laws of nature to the early universe, with the ensuing 'inductive leap' involved in such an extrapolation. The problem was acutely felt already in the 1950s, when, for example, Munitz (1954, p. 42) wrote 'any attempt to apply the generalisations won on the basis of terrestrial experience to vaster regions of space and time and ultimately to the structure of the universe as a whole, requires some justification for extrapolating such generalisations. Here reliance is made on an argument originally due to Mach … '. Curiously enough, the aforementioned Machian argument about the illegitimacy of extrapolating from the current laws to those that might have applied at the origin of our universe, was at the time used by Bondi and other defenders of the steady-state universe to support the perfect cosmological principle, which 'postulates that the universe is homogeneous and stationary in its large-scale appearance as well as in its physical laws' (ibid., p. 43). Only by assuming this perfect cosmological principle, as the latest incarnation of what philosophers of science call the principle of the uniformity of nature, namely that nature is indeed uniform and pretty much the same from any place at any time, could the pressing problem of laws of nature be bypassed. Not surprisingly, however, this line of argument suffers from exactly the same problem of induction that affects the principle of the uniformity of nature: the perfect cosmological principle is itself a universal generalization in need of justification. More to the point, the steady-state universe, within which the perfect cosmological principle was originally formulated, has long been disproved by experimental evidence for an evolving universe from the CMB. Yet this does not mean the end of philosophical reflections on the role of the laws in cosmology. Let us only briefly mention two of the current options.

The first option, discussed by Smeenk (2013, p. 627), is to offer a philosophically more nuanced account of what it is to be a 'law of the universe'. And a closer inspection can soon reveal that cosmological laws are as testable as Newton's laws, even in the early universe, in so far as they give us 'more refined descriptions of some aspect of the universe's history', no matter if we have only one universe and it is given to us once and for all.

The second option, so-called *cosmological natural selection* developed by the physicist Lee Smolin (2013, p. 123) is that 'for cosmology to progress, physics must abandon the idea that laws are timeless and eternal and embrace instead the idea that they evolve in real time'. Once this key step is taken, the problem of explaining why and how the universe came to be governed by our current laws (rather than other possible, different ones) evaporates, and no suspicious inductive leap is required to answer the original question. On Smolin's account, our laws of nature have evolved with us, and our universe. The first of two bonuses of this account, in Smolin's own description, is that a cosmology with evolving laws does not need to rely on the **anthropic principle** (see Chapter 4) to explain why we live in a universe that seems hospitable to forms of life like ours. As in biology life is always evolving and never reaches a final ideal state, similarly our universe is evolving, and so are the laws of nature. The second bonus is that 'the hypothesis of cosmological natural selection makes several genuine predictions, which are falsifiable by currently doable observations' (Smolin 2013, p. 126), e.g. that the biggest neutron stars cannot be heavier than a certain limit. The Popperian flavour of Smolin's hypothesis brings us to our second methodological point, namely the role of Popper's falsification in discussions about the scientific status of cosmology.

Uniqueness and Popper's methodological criterion of falsification

Recall the uniqueness of our universe and the specific problem it poses to the testability of cosmology. Key to our ordinary ideas of what it is like to be a scientific theory is the ability to pass severe tests, tests which are typically run across *multiple samples*, and by tweaking the *circumstances* of the phenomenon we want to investigate. But cosmology has only one object to test and experiment upon, our universe, unique and unrepeatable as it is, and no other objects to compare our universe with. How could cosmology become a scientific discipline, despite the uniqueness of its object of study?

Karl Popper's criterion of **falsification** seems to offer a solution to the problem. As we saw in Chapter 1, Popper believed that the method of science consisted in a deductive method, whereby given a hypothesis or conjecture with *risky novel predictions*, scientists can go about and search for the one single piece of negative evidence that can potentially falsify the hypothesis. Theories that have passed severe tests and have not been falsified, are said to be 'corroborated'. If falsification is indeed the method of science, the uniqueness of our universe does not pose an insurmountable obstacle for cosmology and its scientific status. All that is needed from cosmology is one single risky prediction, which may be tested and proved wrong (what Popper called a potential falsifier).

Thus, on a Popperian approach, the uniqueness of the universe does not really constitute a problem for the scientific status of cosmology, because cosmological theories can indeed make risky and testable predictions (say, the hypothesis of the Big Bang, which implied the existence of CMB, as the last remnant of a hot early phase of the universe, with CMB being experimentally detected in 1965).

Here there is an interesting story to be told, with a surprising twist, about cosmology and Popper's method of falsification (for details about Popper's personal views on cosmology, and some of these debates, see Kragh 2013). In the 1950s, the cosmologist Bondi appealed precisely to the 'uniqueness' of our universe to defend the steady-state universe (namely, the hypothesis of a 'continuous creation' of matter in the universe to explain its expansion). Because there is only one universe, there must have been only one primitive 'substance' of the world emerging, disappearing, and being created again over time during the history of the universe. Funnily enough, Bondi also adamantly defended Popper's method of falsification in cosmology. In an interesting exchange with Whitrow that took place in the *British Journal for the Philosophy of Science* in 1953 (Whitrow and Bondi 1953, pp. 277–8), Bondi asserted that 'the most characteristic feature of any science is that it confines its attention to the establishment of connections between existing results of experiments and observation, and the forecasting of new ones. The chief claim that can be made for any scientific theory is that it fits the facts, and forecasts (or has forecast correctly) the results of new experiments; the chief method of disproof of any theory is that it disagrees with the facts'. Bondi's adherence to Popper's falsificationism was noted by Whitrow, who in his reply qualified falsificationism 'as a method employed in that thoroughgoing pursuit of general unanimity which, in my view, characterizes scientific work' (ibid., p. 280). Whitrow's remarks pointed the finger to the necessity of supplementing falsification with an important sociological, so to speak, aspect of scientific research (i.e. scientific results being unanimously endorsed by a community), to which we'll come back in the next chapter. The interesting final twist of the story is that Bondi's steady-state universe was itself disproved (via the discovery of the CMB in 1965) by the same Popperian method he had hailed. The second, even more ironical twist of the story is that Popper joined these methodological discussions about the scientific status of cosmology, and became (unsurprisingly perhaps) a public supporter of the steady-state universe till the 1980s, when the scientific community had already long dismissed the view (see Kragh 2013 for details).

Observability, indeterminism, and induction

As mentioned at the beginning of this chapter, the third distinctive problem posed by cosmology is the restricted access to what we can observe about our universe. According to the general relativity notion of the past light cone, the *observable universe* is defined as 'the past-light cone of Earth-now, and all physical events within it, even microscopic (and so humanly unobservable) ones' (Butterfield 2014, p. 58). This restricted access to the observability of the universe poses specific problems about the kind of warranted theoretical inferences cosmologists can make about the universe as a whole. The main problem is a form of indeterminism about spacetime. There might be observationally indistinguishable spacetimes (i.e. different models of spacetime, which are nonetheless compatible with the same observable past light cone of events), so that 'locally' an observer looking at the past light cone of their events, will not be able to tell in which spacetime they live. This is a mathematical result originally brought to the general attention by philosophers of physics (Glymour 1977; Malament 1977; Manchak 2009; for a recent discussion see Butterfield 2014). As John Norton (2011) nicely illustrates the problem, we are like ants on an infinite, flat (Euclidean) sheet of paper, who can survey only about a 10,000-square-foot patch, and hence are not able to tell whether the spacetime they inhabit is indeed infinitely flat, or curved like a cylinder with a circumference of 1 mile. This shows what Norton calls also 'the opacity of cosmic inductions', namely the 'absence of warranting facts for inductions in the spacetime case' (Norton 2011, p. 173). Given our past light cone, we might inductively infer to very different, and yet observationally indistinguishable spacetime models, and no facts can make the inference to one of these models more legitimate or warranted than to another model. Norton reports how the considerations usually adduced to bypass this problem seem to appeal to abstract meta-physics and even to **Leibniz's principle of plenitude** and concludes as follows: 'One cannot help but be struck by how tenuous the grounding has become. We are now to secure our inductions in abstract metaphysics. The principle of plenitude itself is sufficiently implausible that we need to prop it up with anthropomorphic metaphors. We are to imagine a personified Nature in the act of creating spacetime. ... [and] supposedly loath to halt with a cubic mile-year of spacetime still uncreated'.

Chapter summary

- For centuries cosmology was regarded as a branch of metaphysics rather than a science. The Kant–Laplace nebular hypothesis at the end of the eighteenth century was one of the first attempts at a scientific explanation of the origins of the universe.
- Cosmology faces three distinct methodological problems as a science: whether our current laws apply to the early universe; the uniqueness of its object of study; and the unobservability of large portions of the universe.
- Progress in the subject has then depended on the large-scale uniformity of the universe. Initially in the form of a guess, this cosmological principle has since been verified over large patches of the currently visible universe.
- Observationally, much of the probing of the distant universe rests on Hubble's law, where the spectroscopic redshift is linearly proportional to distance. The main foundation for this was the pioneering spectroscopy of V. M. Slipher over the decade from 1913.
- Theory played a large part in establishing cosmology. Einstein introduced the idea of a cosmological constant (equivalent to the modern idea of dark energy) in 1917, in order to permit a non-expanding universe, but de Sitter immediately found the first expanding solution, with a prediction of Hubble's law.
- Initially, and until the late 1920s, the non-static nature of the de Sitter model was not appreciated, although this did not prevent astronomers (including Hubble) searching for and finding the 'de Sitter effect'.

Since then, we have viewed cosmological models as describing expanding spacetimes, although the idea of expanding space can lead to misconceptions, since it is not detectable locally.

- Generalization of expanding models to cases containing matter and radiation by Friedman in 1922 and 1924 showed that the origin of the expansion lay in a singularity at a finite time in the past – the Big Bang. With the discovery of the CMB (cosmic microwave background) in 1965, this hot origin for the universe became the accepted picture.
- The main constituents of the universe are *dark matter* and *dark energy*. The former is a form of matter that can clump, but which does not support sound waves; the latter is effectively an energy density associated with empty space, which causes a tendency for the expansion of the universe to accelerate.
- The early universe should be hot, and dominated by the density of relativistic particles. This leads to the prediction of the CMB, when the universe cooled sufficiently to become neutral.
- The radiation-dominated universe must emerge from a singularity in the Big Bang, only a finite time in the past. It is impossible to ask what came before such a time, and yet the universe at this point must be set up in a special uniform state. It should also contain small fluctuations in the curvature of spacetime in order to seed the future formation of galaxies and other astronomical structures.
- Two possible ways of overcoming the problem with laws in cosmology are either by revising our philosophical intuitions about the testability of the laws, or by assuming that the laws evolve and change over time with our universe.
- Despite there being only one object to study, the universe, cosmology seems amenable to Popper's method of falsification, whereby evidence coming from the CMB eventually falsified the hypothesis of the steady-state universe.
- The restriction of observability to the past light cone of events means that there might well be many observationally indistinguishable spacetimes and any inductive inference from available data to the exact nature of the spacetime we live in is inevitably unwarranted.

Study questions

1 Why was cosmology regarded as a branch of metaphysics in the eighteenth century?
2 What was Kant's contribution to the history of cosmology?
3 What is the problem with laws in cosmology?
4 Why does the uniqueness of our universe pose a problem for cosmology as a science?
5 Can you clarify the exact nature of the problem of unobservability in cosmology?
6 Explain the meaning of 'telescopes are time machines'.

7 Why do we expect that the density of the universe will be dominated by radiation at sufficiently early times?

8 Radiation from sufficiently great distances originates from plasma at temperatures of over 1,000 degrees. Why then is it dark at night?

9 Does the history of cosmology show that Popper's falsificationism is the right scientific method?

10 Can you explain what Norton means by 'the opacity of cosmic inductions'?

Introductory further reading

Beisbart, C. and Jung, T. (2006) 'Privileged, typical or not even that? Our place in the world according to the Copernican and cosmological principles', *Journal for General Philosophy of Science* 40: 225–56.

Brush, S. G. (1996) *A History of Modern Planetary Physics: Nebulous Earth*, Cambridge: Cambridge University Press. (A good introduction to the history of the Kant–Laplace nebular hypothesis up to the early twentieth century.)

Ellis, G. F. R. (2014) 'On the philosophy of cosmology', *Studies in History and Philosophy of Modern Physics* 46: 5–23.

Guth, A. H. (1998) *The Inflationary Universe: The Quest for a New Theory of Cosmic Origins*, London: Vintage. (This is a very good introduction to inflationary cosmology, written by one of the creators of the theory.)

Kragh, H. (2013) '"The most philosophically important of all the sciences": Karl Popper and physical cosmology', *Perspectives on Science* 21: 325–57.

Liddle, A. R. (2003) *An Introduction to Modern Cosmology*, Malden, MA: Wiley-Blackwell. (An introductory undergraduate text for non-specialists.)

Massimi, M. (2013) 'Are scientific theories true?', in M. Chrisman and D. Pritchard (eds) *Philosophy for Everyone*, London: Routledge.

Munitz, M. K. (1954) 'Creation and the "new" cosmology', *British Journal for the Philosophy of Science* 5: 32–46.

Norton, J. (2011) 'Observationally indistinguishable spacetimes: a challenge for any inductivist', in G. J. Morgan (ed.) *Philosophy of Science Matters: The Philosophy of Peter Achinstein*, Oxford: Oxford University Press, pp. 164–76. (An excellent paper that explains the physics and the philosophy behind indistinguishable spacetimes in a very clear and accessible way.)

Sklar, L. (1974) *Space, Time, and Spacetime*, Berkeley: University of California Press. (An excellent introduction to a variety of philosophical aspects concerning theories of space and time.)

Smolin, L. (2013) *Time Reborn*, London: Penguin Books.

Whitrow, G. J. (1954) 'The age of the universe', *British Journal for the Philosophy of Science* 5: 215–25.

Whitrow, G. J. and Bondi, H. (1953) 'Is physical cosmology a science?', *British Journal for the Philosophy of Science* 4: 271–83.

Advanced further reading

Butterfield, J. (2014) 'On under-determination in cosmology', *Studies in History and Philosophy of Modern Physics* 46: 57–69. (An excellent introduction to the problem of observationally indistinguishable spacetimes by a world-leading philosopher of physics.)

Glymour, C. (1977) 'Indistinguishable spacetimes and the fundamental group', in J. Earman, C. Glymour and J. Stachel (eds) *Foundations of Spacetime Theories*, Minnesota Studies in Philosophy of Science 8, Minneapolis: University of Minnesota Press, pp. 50–60.

Malament, D. (1977) 'Observationally indistinguishable spacetimes', in J. Earman, C. Glymour and J. Stachel (eds) *Foundations of Spacetime Theories*, Minnesota Studies in Philosophy of Science 8, Minneapolis: University of Minnesota Press, 61–80.

Manchak, J. (2009) 'Can we know the global structure of spacetime?', *Studies in History and Philosophy of Modern Physics* 40: 53–56.

Peacock, J. A. (1999) *Cosmological Physics*, Cambridge: Cambridge University Press. (This is a comprehensive postgraduate text covering most areas of modern cosmology.)

Smeenk, C. (2013) 'Philosophy of cosmology', in R. Batterman (ed.) *The Oxford Handbook of Philosophy of Physics*, Oxford University Press, pp. 607–52. (This is an excellent introductory chapter to some of the main philosophical trends by a leading expert in the field.)

Way, M. and Hunter, D. (eds) (2013) *Origins of the Expanding Universe: 1912–1932*, Astronomical Society of the Pacific Conference Series, vol. 471, San Francisco: Astronomical Society of the Pacific. (A meeting held in September 2012 to mark the Centenary of Slipher's first measurement of the radial velocity of M31.)

Internet resources

John Templeton Foundation (n.d.) *Philosophy of Cosmology*, Oxford University [website] www.philosophy-of-cosmology.ox.ac.uk (accessed 26 May 2014) (This is the official website of the Templeton-funded project on philosophy of cosmology, based at Oxford and Cambridge University. It provides useful links to key concepts and podcasts of events and lectures.)

John Templeton Foundation (n.d.) *Rutgers Templeton Project in Philosophy of Cosmology*, Rutgers School of Arts and Sciences, Rutgers University [website] http://philocosmol ogy.rutgers.edu (accessed 26 May 2014) (This is the equivalent counterpart of the Templeton-funded project at Rutgers University. It contains a very helpful blog too.)

Peacock, J. A. (2013) 'MPhys advanced cosmology', University of Edinburgh [online lecture notes], www.roe.ac.uk/japwww/teaching/

Wright, N. (n.d.) *Cosmological Tutorial*, UCLA Division of Astronomy and Astrophysics [website], www.astro.ucla.edu/~wright/cosmolog.htm (accessed 9 June 2014) (A wide-ranging overview of many issues in cosmology. Simplified for a general audience, but far from simplistic.)

3 What are dark matter and dark energy?

Michela Massimi and John Peacock

Introduction: rationality of theory choice and underdetermination of theory by evidence

Cosmology has established itself as a successful scientific discipline in its own right, as we saw in the previous chapter. But contemporary cosmological research faces new pressing philosophical challenges. The current cosmological model, the so-called 'concordance model' or ΛCDM – which builds on Einstein's general-relativity (GR) and the so-called Friedmann–Lemaître–Robertson–Walker (FLRW) models – maintains that we live in an infinite universe, with approximately 5 per cent ordinary matter (baryons), 25 per cent cold dark matter, and 70 per cent dark energy. According to this picture, the vast majority of our universe is populated by two exotic entities, called dark matter (DM) and dark energy (DE). While the search for experimental evidence for DM and DE is at the forefront of contemporary research in cosmology, from a philosophical point of view we should ask how scientists came to believe in the existence of these two new kinds of entities, and their reasons and justification for this view. What are DE and DM? How justified are we in believing in them?

The philosophical debate behind these central questions concerns the rationality of theory choice. What reasons do scientists have for choosing one scientific theory over a rival one? How do we go about making rational choices when there is more than one candidate that seems compatible with the same experimental evidence? The history of physics offers an embarrassment of riches in this respect (see Lahav and Massimi 2014). Consider, for example, the discovery of the planet Neptune back in 1846. The anomalous perihelion of the planet Uranus was known for some time, and two astronomers Urbain Le Verrier and John Couch Adams, independently of each other, tried to reconcile this observed conflict with Newtonian theory by postulating the existence of a new planet,[1] called Neptune, whose orbit and mass interfered with and explained the anomalous orbit of Uranus. The new planet was indeed observed on 23 September 1846, the actual position having been independently predicted with a good degree of accuracy by both Adams and Le Verrier. A very similar phenomenon was also observed for the planet Mercury. Also in this case

Le Verrier postulated the existence of a new planet, Vulcan, to explain the observed anomaly. But this time the predicted planet was not found, and a final explanation of the phenomenon came only with the advent of GR.

Or, to take another example, consider the negative evidence for ether drag in the Michelson–Morley experiment of 1887. The experiment used an interferometer, which was designed to record the velocity of two orthogonal beams of light at different angles to the direction of the Earth's motion through the presumed ether (via slight changes in their interference patterns). But no such changes in the interference patterns were ever observed. Rather than abandoning altogether the hypothesis of the ether, however, scientists tried to reconcile this piece of negative evidence with Newtonian mechanics (and the hypothesis of the ether) by assuming a contraction of length to occur in the interferometer arm (the so-called Lorentz–Fitzgerald contraction hypothesis). A final conclusive explanation of this piece of negative evidence came only in 1905 when the young Albert Einstein introduced the special theory of relativity, which overthrew the Newtonian assumption that the velocity of light is dependent on the frame of reference employed (the assumption that underpinned the very search for ether drag in the Michelson–Morley experiment).

These two historical examples illustrate a phenomenon that we have already encountered in Chapter 1, namely underdetermination of theory by evidence: in the presence of more than one possible scientific theory or hypothesis, the available experimental evidence may underdetermine the choice among them. In other words, experimental evidence per se may not be sufficient to determine the choice for one scientific theory or hypothesis over a rival one (e.g. that there is a new planet, as opposed to Newtonian mechanics being false). To understand underdetermination of theory by evidence, we need to bear in mind what we discussed in Chapter 1 about Pierre Duhem's observation (1906/1991) that a scientific hypothesis is never tested in isolation, but always with a collection of other main theoretical and auxiliary hypotheses. For example, to use again the case of Uranus, the anomalous perihelion was evidence that something was wrong with the set of hypotheses including both *main theoretical assumptions* about Newtonian mechanics and *auxiliary hypotheses* about the number of planets, their masses, sizes, and orbits. But the anomaly per se does not tell us which of these (main or auxiliary) hypotheses is the culprit for the anomaly. Thus, if an anomaly is found, the question naturally arises of whether we should reject or modify one of the main theoretical hypotheses (i.e. Newtonian mechanics and its laws), or tweak and add one auxiliary hypothesis (i.e. change the number of planets in the solar system). And, as the similar case of the anomalous perihelion of Mercury shows, finding the right answer to this kind of question may well be far from obvious. Duhem concluded that scientists typically follow their 'good sense' in making decisions in such situations.

Even if 'good sense' might be the most fairly distributed thing among human beings (as Descartes used to say), Duhem's answer to the problem of the rationality of theory choice is not satisfactory. For one thing, it is not clear what 'good sense' is, nor why scientists X's good sense should lead them to agree with scientists Y's good sense. Worse, it delegates the rationality of theory choice to whatever a scientific community might deem the 'most sensible' choice to make, even if that choice may well be the wrong one. Not surprisingly perhaps, Duhem's problem of underdetermination of theory by evidence was expanded upon, fifty years or so later, by the American philosopher W. V. O. Quine (1951), who showed the far-reaching implications of the view and concluded by appealing to what he called 'entrenchment'. In Quine's view, as we discussed in Chapter 1, our hypotheses form a web of beliefs that impinges on experience along the edges and where every single belief, including the most stable ones of logic and mathematics, are subject to the 'tribunal of experience', and can be revised at any point. What confers stability to some beliefs more than others, more peripheral ones in the web, is simply their 'entrenchment' within the web. One may wonder at this point why these observations about the nature of scientific theories, and how scientists go about choosing and revising them, should pose a problem for the rationality of theory choice. This is where the argument from underdetermination is typically employed to draw anti-realist conclusions about science. Let us then see the argument in more detail, and why it poses a problem.

The argument from underdetermination to the threat to the rationality of theory choice proceeds from three premises (see Kukla 1996):

1 Scientists' belief in a theory T_1 is justified (i.e. they have good reasons for believing that theory T_1 is *true*)
2 Scientific theory T_1 has to be read literally (i.e. if the theory talks about planetary motions, we must take what the theory says about planetary motions *at face value*)
3 T_1 is *empirically equivalent* to another theory T_2 when T_1 and T_2 have the same empirical consequences.

Therefore premise 1 must be false.

To appreciate the strength of the argument here, let us go back to our example about the observed anomalous perihelion of Mercury in the nineteenth century. Astronomers had sufficient data and measurements to be sure of the existence of this anomalous phenomenon. They also had very good reasons for (1) believing that Newtonian mechanics (T_1) was the *true* or correct theory about planetary motions: after all, Newton's theory was the best available theory back then; it had proved very successful over the past century, and had also been further confirmed by the recent discovery of the planet Neptune. Astronomers also (2) took what Newtonian mechanics (T_1) said about planetary motions at *face value*. For example, if the theory said that given the mass of Mercury and its orbit around the sun, we should expect to observe the perihelion of Mercury (the closest point to the sun during its orbit) to be subject to a slight rotation or precession, and this precession to be of the order of 5,557 seconds of arc per century, then given premise 2 astronomers took the 5,557 seconds of arc per century *to be the case*. Hence, the observed discrepancy of 43 seconds of arc per century from the predicted figure of 5,557 became the anomalous phenomenon in need of explanation.

But, to complicate things, suppose that in addition to Newtonian mechanics (T_1) a new theory comes to the fore, Einstein's GR (T_2), and these two theories prove empirically equivalent as far as the *anomalous perihelion of Mercury* (let us call it APM) is concerned. Being *empirically equivalent* here means that both T_1 and T_2 *imply* or *entail* the same empirical consequence, e.g. APM. In other words, we can deduce APM from *either* Newtonian mechanics (plus the auxiliary hypothesis of a new planet, Vulcan, having a certain mass and orbit which interferes with Mercury's) *or* from GR (i.e. the anomalous 43 seconds of Mercury follows from Einstein's field equations). Thus, it follows that if we take Newtonian mechanics and its predictions of 5,557 seconds for the precession of Mercury *at face value*, and there is another theory (GR) that can *equally* account for the same anomaly about Mercury's perihelion, we have no more overwhelming reasons for retaining Newtonian mechanics as the *true* theory than we have for taking GR as the true theory instead. This is the threat that the underdetermination argument poses to the rationality of theory choice.

We can now say 'Of course, that was the sign that Newtonian mechanics was false, after all'. But back in the nineteenth century when the anomaly was first discovered, and before scientific consensus gathered around Einstein's relativity theory in the early twentieth century, one might reasonably conclude that the rationality of theory choice was in fact underdetermined by evidence. Why should it have been 'rational' for astronomers at the beginning of the century to abandon Newtonian mechanics in favour of GR? Were not the reasons on both sides *equally* good, *back then*?

We can then appreciate the anti-realist conclusions that seem to follow from the underdetermination argument. Scientific realism is the view that science aims to give us with its theories a *literally true story* of what the world is like (van Fraassen 1980). If the underdetermination argument above is correct, then scientific realism is in trouble: given any two empirically equivalent theories, we seem to have no more reason for taking one of them to be *more likely to be the case* than the other. Indeed, neither may be true. Newtonian mechanics is not the way the world really functions – but it is often convenient to think about matters as though Newtonian mechanics were true, because we know it is an accurate approximation within well-understood regimes of validity. Thus, the underdetermination argument challenges the claim that in theory choice there are *objectively good reasons* for choosing one (more likely to be true) theory over a (less likely to be true) rival. Not surprisingly, as we saw in Chapter 1, these anti-realist considerations resonate in the work of the influential historian and philosopher of science Thomas Kuhn (1962/1996). Kuhn dismantled the scientific realist picture of science as triumphantly marching towards the *truth* by accumulating a sequences of theories that build on their predecessors and *are more and more likely to be true* the closer we come to contemporary science. Kuhn's profound commitment to the history of science led him to debunk this irenic picture of how scientific inquiry grows and unfolds, and to replace it with a new cyclic picture, whereby science goes through periods of normal science, crises and scientific revolutions.

Although Kuhn never formulated the underdetermination argument as above, he clearly subscribed to some version of this argument. For example, he claimed that theory choice, far from being a rational and objective exercise, is indeed affected by external, contextual considerations including the beliefs and system of values of a given community at a given historical time (captured by Kuhn's notion of scientific paradigm). In his 1977 work, Kuhn pointed out that theory choice seems indeed governed by five objective criteria: *accuracy* (i.e. the theory is in agreement with experimental evidence); *consistency* (i.e. the theory is consistent with other accepted scientific theories); *broad scope* (i.e. the theory has to go beyond the original phenomena it was designed to explain); *simplicity* (i.e. the theory should give a simple account of the phenomena); and *fruitfulness* (i.e. the theory should be able to predict novel phenomena). Yet, Kuhn continued, these criteria are either imprecise (e.g. how to define 'simplicity'?) or they conflict with one another (e.g. while Copernicanism seems preferable to Ptolemaic astronomy on the basis of accuracy, consistency would pick out Ptolemaic astronomy given its consistency with the Aristotelean–Archimedean tradition at the time). Kuhn thus reaches the anti-realist conclusion that these five joint criteria are not sufficient to determine theory choice at any given time, and instead external, sociological factors seem to play a decisive role in theory choice (e.g. Kepler's adherence to Neoplatonism seems to have been a factor in leading him to endorse Copernicanism). It is no surprise that, rightly or wrongly, Kuhn's reflections on theory choice opened the door to Feyerabend's (1975) **methodological anarchism** and to what became later known as the sociology of scientific knowledge.

This is not the place for us to enter into a discussion of the sociological ramifications of Kuhn's view. Instead, going back to our topic in this chapter, we should ask what the evidence is for the current standard cosmological model, and whether in this case there might also be *empirically equivalent* rivals. We are at a key juncture in the history of cosmology: the search for DE and DM is still ongoing, with several large spectroscopic and photometric galaxy surveys either under way. In a few years down the line, we will be able to know whether the anomalous phenomena of an accelerating expansion of the universe, and flat galaxy rotation curves, are indeed the signs for the existence of DE and DM – or whether we should actually abandon the framework of relativity theory (the FLRW models). In the next section, we review the scientific evidence for DE and DM, as well as some of their proposed rivals to date. In the final section, we return to the underdetermination problem and the rationality of theory choice and we assess the prospects and promises of the current standard cosmological model.

Dark matter and dark energy

Modern observations tell us much about the universe globally (its expansion history) and locally (development of structure). But making a consistent picture from all this information is only possible with the introduction of two new ingredients: DM and DE. To understand what these are, we must look at the Friedmann equation. This governs the time dependence of the **scale factor** of the universe, $R(t)$. Separations between all galaxies increase in proportion to $R(t)$, and its absolute value is the length scale over which we must take into account spacetime curvature. The equation is astonishingly simple, and resembles classical conservation of energy: $[dR(t)/dt]^2 - (8\pi G/3) \rho(t) R(t)^2 = -K$, where G is the gravitational constant, ρ is the total mass density, and K is a constant. One deep result from Einstein's relativistic theory of gravity is that K is related to the curvature of spacetime, i.e. whether the universe is open (infinite: negative K) or closed (finite: positive K). This says that the universe expands faster if you increase the density, or if you make the curvature more negative. Because the universe is inevitably denser at early times, curvature is unimportant early on. This means that, if we can measure the rate of expansion today and in the past, then we can infer both the density of the universe and its curvature.

In practice, we can match observations using Friedmann's equation only if $K = 0$, and if the density, ρ, is larger than expected based on ordinary visible matter. There must be DM, with a density about five times that of normal matter, and dark energy (a poor name), which is distinguished by being uniformly distributed (unlike other matter, which clumps). The universe appears to be dominated by DE, which contributes about 70 per cent of the total density.

This standard cosmological picture is called the **ΛCDM model**, standing for Λ (the cosmological constant) plus cold dark matter ('cold' here implies that the dark matter has negligible random motion, as if it were a gas at low temperature). The claim that the universe is dominated by two unusual components is certainly cause for some scepticism, so it is worth a brief summary of why this is widely believed to be a correct description. The main point to stress is that the ΛCDM model can be arrived at by using a number of lines of evidence and different classes of argument. Removing any single piece of evidence reduces the accuracy with which the cosmological parameters are known, but does not change the basic form of the conclusion: this has been the standard cosmological framework since the 1990s, and it has witnessed a great improvement in the quality and quantity of data without coming under serious challenge. If the model is wrong, this would require an implausible conspiracy between a number of completely independent observations. It is impossible in a short space to list all the methods that have contributed, but the two main types of approach are as follows.

The easiest to understand is based on **standard candles**, or **standard rulers**. If we populate the universe with identical objects, their relative distances can be inferred. Suppose we have two copies of the same object, A and B, where

B is twice as far from us as *A*. Object *B* will subtend half the angle that *A* does, and we will receive energy from it at a rate that is four times smaller (the inverse-square law). Finding identical objects is hard: the angular sizes of the sun and moon are very similar, but the moon is a small nearby object, whereas the sun is much larger and more distant. But suppose that standard objects can be found, and that we can also measure their redshifts: these relate to the distance via Hubble's law, but because we are looking into the past, we need the rate of expansion as it was in the past, and this depends on the contents of the universe. A universe containing only matter will have a much higher density in the past compared with one dominated by DE, where the density appears not to change with time. In the latter case, then, the expansion rate will be lower at early times for a given distance; alternatively, for a given redshift (which is all we observe directly) the distance will be larger at early times (and hence objects will appear fainter), if DE dominates. This is exactly what was seen around 1998 with the use of Type Ia supernovae. These exploding stars are not quite identical objects (their masses vary), but the more luminous events shine for longer, so they can be corrected into standard objects that yield relative distances to about 5 per cent precision. By now, hundreds of these events have been accurately studied, so that the overall distance–redshift relation is very precisely measured, and the evidence for DE seems very strong. This work was honoured with the 2011 Nobel Prize.

But although supernova cosmology is a very direct method, the first strong evidence for DE was in place at the start of the 1990s, on the basis of the information contained in the large-scale structure of the universe (see Figure 3.1).

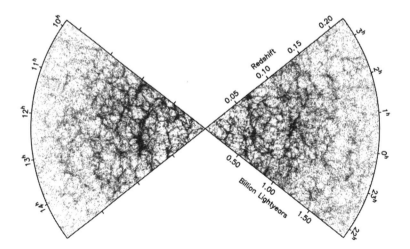

Figure 3.1 The large-scale structure of the universe, as revealed in the distribution of the galaxies by the 2-degree Field Galaxy Redshift Survey. The chains of galaxies stretching over hundreds of millions of light years represent the action of gravity concentrating small initial density irregularities that were created in the earliest stages of the expanding universe. (Copyright photo: John Peacock)

The fluctuations in density that we see in the CMB (cosmic microwave background) and in large-scale galaxy clustering contain a standard length, which is set by the time when the universe passed through the era of 'matter–radiation equality'. What this means is that the density of the universe was dominated at early times by relativistic particles such as photons, but as the universe expands and cools, non-relativistic matter (DM plus normal matter) becomes more important (see Figure 3.2).

This is useful in two ways: the transition scale depends on the matter density, so it is a useful means of 'weighing' the universe, and determining the matter density. But the scale can also be seen at high redshift in the CMB, and so again we are sensitive to the change in the expansion rate at high redshift. Combining galaxy clustering with the CMB in this way already strongly pointed to the need for DE as early as 1990. There is an interesting

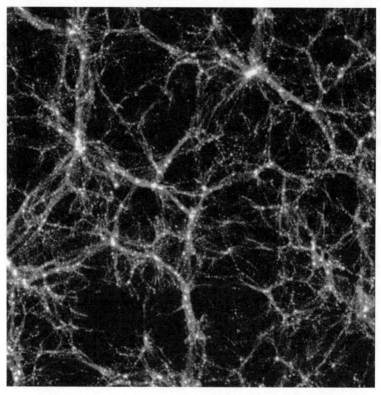

Figure 3.2 A slice through a computer simulation of structure formation in a standard-model universe, dominated by dark matter and dark energy. The scale of the image is approximately 650 million light years on a side. The dark matter clumps under gravity, generating a network of filaments and voids that bears a striking resemblance to the structure seen in the real galaxy distribution, as illustrated in Figure 3.1. (Copyright photo: John Peacock)

sociological point here, namely that the 1990 evidence did not meet with immediate acceptance. This is not so much because the arguments were weak, but because many researchers (including one of the current authors) were reluctant to believe that the density of the vacuum really could be non-zero (the physical problems with this are discussed below). But the 1998 supernova results were accepted almost immediately, and ΛCDM became the standard model. Those who were reluctant to accept a non-zero Λ now had to search for reasons why two such different arguments should conspire to yield the same conclusion; most workers found this implausible, and so the consensus shifted.

The explanation for DM need not be particularly radical. It is plausibly an exotic massive particle left as a relic of early times (in the same way as the photons of the CMB, or the nuclei resulting from primordial nucleosynthesis). Such a particle would be collisionless (i.e. it would not support sound waves in the same way as ordinary gas), and there is good evidence that DM has this character. There are a number of ways in which this conjecture could be tested, most directly by seeing the relic DM particles interacting in the laboratory. Although these **WIMPs** (weakly interacting massive particles) are by definition hard to detect other than via gravity, they will suffer occasional rare collisions with normal particles. The challenge is to distinguish such events from the background of less exotic processes, and consequently the direct-detection experiments operate many kilometres underground, using the Earth itself to shield out potential contaminants such as cosmic rays. If relic WIMPs can be detected, we may also hope to make new particles of the same properties in accelerators (pre-eminently the LHC 'Large Hadron Collider' at CERN). So far, neither route has yielded sight of a new particle, but it remains plausible that detection could happen within the next few years.

A third indirect route exploits the fact that WIMPs will also interact weakly with themselves: relic WIMPs and anti-WIMPs should exist in equal numbers, and the relics are those particles that failed to annihilate at an earlier stage of the universe. In regions of high density, such as the centres of galaxies, annihilations could continue at a sufficient rate to generate detectable radiation in the form of gamma rays. Indeed, there have been tantalizing signals reported in the past few years by NASA's Fermi gamma-ray observatory, which could be exactly this signal. But other sources of gamma-ray emission are possible, so this route does not yet prove the WIMP hypothesis for DM.

In contrast, DE seems hardly a form of matter at all: it behaves as if it were simply an energy density of a vacuum – a property of 'empty' space that remains unchanged as the universe expands. Although this sounds contradictory, it is easy to show from the **uncertainty principle** that an exactly zero vacuum density would not be expected. This argument goes back to the early days of quantum mechanics and the attempt to understand the form of black-body radiation. Planck's solution was to envisage the space inside an empty box as being filled with electromagnetic wave modes, each of which can be excited in steps of energy $E = h\nu$, where h is Planck's constant and ν is the frequency of the mode, each step corresponding to the creation of one photon. The black-body spectrum cuts off at high frequencies because eventually $h\nu$ becomes larger than a typical thermal energy, and therefore not even one photon can typically be created. But Einstein and Stern realized in 1913 that Planck's original expression for the energy of an oscillator was wrong: instead of $E = n\,h\nu$ for n photons, it should be $E = (n + 1/2)\,h\nu$, adding a constant **zero-point energy** that is present even in the vacuum ($n = 0$). It is impressive that this is more than a decade before Heisenberg showed that the zero-point energy was predicted by the new uncertainty principle in quantum mechanics. This states that the uncertainty in position (x) and in the momentum of a particle (p, which stands for mass $\times$ velocity) is in the form of a product: $\delta x\ \delta p =$ constant. Thus it is impossible for a particle to be completely at rest, as both its position and momentum would be perfectly known. Similarly, a perfectly still electromagnetic field is impossible. By 1916, Nernst had realized that the energy density of the vacuum therefore diverged, unless a maximum frequency for electromagnetic radiation was imposed. Cutting off at an X-ray frequency of 10^{20} Hz gave Nernst a vacuum density of 100 times that of water, which seemed puzzlingly high even then. This problem is still with us today.

The gravitational effects of this vacuum density are identical to those of a leading feature of cosmology: the cosmological constant introduced by Einstein in 1917. In effect, the cosmological constant and the density of zero-point energy add together into one effective density of DE (to which there can be further contributions, as we will see). As mentioned in Chapter 2, Einstein added the cosmological constant to his gravitational field equations in order to achieve a static universe. This is possible because DE in effect displays **antigravity**, i.e. its gravitational force is repulsive when the density is positive. This unexpected property can be deduced from the fact that DE does not dilute with expansion. For normal matter, doubling the size of the universe increases the volume by a factor of 8, so the density declines to 1/8th its initial size; but no such effect is seen with DE. This fact means that the mass inside a sphere of vacuum increases as the sphere expands, rather than remaining constant – so that it becomes more gravitationally bound, requiring an increase in kinetic energy to balance.

Conversely, for normal matter the gravitational effects decline in importance as the expansion progresses, leading to a decelerating expansion. In the past, the density of normal matter was higher, and so the universe is expected to have started out in a decelerating expansion. But today we live in a universe where the density of DE outbalances that of DM plus visible matter by a ratio of roughly 70:30, which means that the gravitational repulsion of DE dominates, yielding an **accelerating universe**. By the time the universe is twice its current age, it will have settled almost exactly into a vacuum-dominated exponentially expanding state – the very same one discovered by de Sitter in 1917.

Clearly it is impressive that we can account quantitatively for so many different astronomical observations using a standard model with relatively few ingredients. It can also be seen as a tribute to the science of astronomy that it was able to reveal such a fundamental ingredient of the universe as DE. But in a sense these achievements of modern cosmology have been obtained illegally. The basic laws of physics have been obtained entirely from experiments carried out on Earth – on characteristic length scales ranging from perhaps 1,000 km to subnuclear scales ($\sim 10^{-15}$ m). Although observational support for these laws thus covers over 20 powers of 10, the largest observable cosmological scales are 20 powers of 10 again larger than the Earth, so it is a considerable extrapolation to assume that no new physics exists that only manifests itself on very large scales. Nevertheless, this is how cosmologists choose to play the game: otherwise, it is impossible to make any predictions for cosmological observations. If this approach fails, we are clearly in trouble: ad hoc new pieces of cosmological physics can be invented to account for any observation whatsoever. Nevertheless, a significant number of scientists do indeed take the view that the need for DM and DE in effect says that standard physics does not work on astronomical scales, and that we should consider more radical alternatives.

One option is MOND: modified Newtonian dynamics. By changing the Newtonian equation of motion in the limit of ultra-low accelerations, one can remove the need for DM in matching internal dynamics of galaxies. Although the most precise evidence for DM is now to be found in large-scale clustering, the first clear evidence did emerge from galaxy dynamics, particularly the observation of 'flat rotation curves': the speed at which gas orbits at different distances from the centres of galaxies can be measured, and is generally found to stay nearly constant at large radii. This is puzzling if we consider only visible matter: for orbits beyond the edge of the starlight, the enclosed mass should be constant and the rotation speed should fall. The fact that this is not seen appears to show that the enclosed mass continues to grow, implying that galaxies are surrounded by halos of invisible matter. Within the standard ΛCDM model, this is certainly not a surprise: computer simulation of gravitational collapse from generic random initial conditions reveals that DM automatically arranges itself in nearly spherical blobs, and the gas from which stars are made is inevitably attracted to the centres of these objects.

Nevertheless, it is empirically disturbing that DM only seems to show itself in galaxies when we are far from the centres, so that the accelerations are lower than the regime in which Newton's $F = m\,a$ has ever been tested. If this law changes at low accelerations in a universal way, it is possible to achieve impressive success in matching the data on galaxy rotation without invoking DM; and MOND proponents claim that their fits are better than those predicted in models with DM. Indeed, there is a long-standing problem with explaining dwarf galaxies, which are apparently dominated by DM everywhere, and so should be able to be compared directly to DM simulations. The inferred density profiles lack the sharp central cusp that is predicted from gravitational collapse – so these models are apparently ruled out at a basic level. But most cosmologists have yet to reject the DM hypothesis, for reasons that can be understood via **Bayes' theorem** in statistics.

The probability of a theory is a product of the prior degree of belief in the theory and the probability of the theory accounting for a given set of data: when the prior belief for DM is strong (as it is here, given the success in accounting for the CMB, for example), there must be extremely strong reasons for rejecting the hypothesis of DM. Also, we need to bear in mind that it is easy to reject a theory spuriously by making excessive simplifications in the modelling used to compare with data. In the case of dwarf galaxies, normal (baryonic) matter is almost entirely absent, even though on average it makes up 20 per cent of the cosmic matter content. Therefore, some violent event early in the evolution of the dwarfs must have removed the gas, and could therefore plausibly have disturbed the DM. Until such effects are modelled with realistic sophistication, cosmologists are rightly reluctant to reject a theory on the basis of possibly simplistic modelling.

The problem with MOND, on the other hand, is that it seemed ad hoc and non-relativistic – so that it was impossible to say what the consequences for the cosmological expansion would be. Bekenstein removed this objection in 2004, when he introduced a relativistic version of MOND. His model was part of a broader class of efforts to construct theories of **modified gravity**. Such theories gain part of their motivation from DE, which manifests itself as the need to introduce a constant density into the Friedmann equation in order to yield accelerating expansion. But perhaps the Friedmann equation may itself be wrong. It derives from Einstein's relativistic gravitational theory, and a different theory would modify Friedmann's equation. On this view, DE could be an illusion caused by the wrong theory for gravity. How can we tell the difference?

The answer is that gravity not only affects the overall expansion of the universe, but also the formation of structure (voids and superclusters) within it. Therefore, much current research effort goes into trying to measure the rate of growth of such density perturbations, and asking if they are consistent with standard gravity plus the existence of DE as a real physical substance. Currently, at the 10 per cent level of precision, this test is passed. This consistency check is pleasing and important: previous generations of cosmologists took without question the assumption that Einstein's approach to gravity was the correct one; but such fundamental assumptions should be capable of being challenged and probed empirically.

What prospects for contemporary cosmology?

Going back then to the underdetermination problem and the rationality of theory choice, we may ask to what extent the current concordance model ΛCDM is well supported by the available evidence. The story told in the second section ('Dark Matter and Dark Energy') shows already how the hypothesis of DE met with a certain resistance in the scientific community in the early

1990s, when the first main evidence for it came from large-scale galaxy clustering. Only in 1998, when supernova Ia data became available as further evidence, did the scientific community come to endorse the idea of an energy density of the vacuum that manifests itself as a form of antigravity or repulsion. (Kant, who, as we saw in Chapter 2, believed in a counterbalance between attraction and repulsion as the mechanism at work in the constitution of the universe, would be delighted to hear that his intuitions seem vindicated by the idea of a repulsive antigravity outbalancing DM and baryonic matter.) The reluctance of the scientific community to embrace the hypothesis of DE back in the 1990s might be explained by the exotic nature of the entity (that 'empty' space can have a non-zero energy density still feels wrong to many physicists, even though they know how to derive the result). Here we find replicated Duhem's story about how a piece of negative or anomalous evidence does not unequivocally speak against a main theoretical assumption, but may instead argue in favour of an additional auxiliary hypothesis. Under-determination looms again on the horizon, as Table 3.1 shows (adapted from Lahav and Massimi 2014).

If the underdetermination argument is correct, the choice between the ΛCDM model vs its rivals would not seem to be on rational grounds. Indeed, one might be tempted to bring in sociological explanations behind scientists gathering their consensus around the standard cosmological model rather than its rivals. For example, one might argue that it is easier to hold onto an accepted and well-established theory such as GR (plus DE) than trying to modify it (nor do we currently possess a well-established alternative to GR). And even in those cases where we do have a well-worked out alternative (such as MOND), one might be tempted to hold onto the accepted theory (plus DM), on grounds of the ad hoc nature of the modification of Newton's second law involved in MOND. Are scientists following again their 'good sense' in making these decisions? And what counts as 'good sense' here? After all, MOND supporters would argue that their theory is very successful in explaining not only galaxy rotation curves (without resorting to DM) but also other cosmological phenomena. From *their* point of view, 'good sense' would recommend taking relativistic MOND seriously.

To give an answer to these pressing questions at the forefront of con-temporary research in cosmology, we should then examine first the premise of empirical equivalence in the underdetermination argument. After all, as we

Table 3.1

Anomaly	Reject a main theoretical assumption?	Add a new auxiliary hypothesis?
Galaxy flat rotation curves	Modify Newtonian dynamics (MOND)?	Halos of dark matter?
Accelerating universe	Modify GR? Retain GR, modify FLRW?	Dark energy?

saw in the introductory section, this premise is the culprit of the argument itself. In the next section, we review both the physical data behind the prima facie empirical equivalence between the standard cosmological model and its rivals, and draw some philosophical considerations about this debate and the challenge to the rationality of theory choice.

Empirical equivalence between ΛCDM and rival theories?

Let us then look a bit more closely to some of the rivals to the current ΛCDM model, starting with DE. Critics of DE typically complain on two main grounds: first, the lack of *direct empirical evidence* for DE as of today; and second, lack of understanding of why the vacuum would have a non-zero energy density. The first problem is admittedly real, as we have only inferred the existence of DE via the fact of the accelerating expansion of the universe. Future experiments, e.g. the Dark Energy Survey, will have mapped 200 million galaxies by 2018, using four different probes, with the aim of measuring the signature of DE precisely, but they will only at best show that the acceleration is measured consistently: we do not expect to *touch* DE. The second worry is also difficult to dismiss, and is of a more philosophical nature. Critics complain about what seems to be the ad hoc introduction of DE into the current cosmological model, as the latest incarnation of Einstein's infamous cosmological constant (i.e. tweak a parameter, give a non-zero value to it, and accommodate in this way the theory to the evidence). Dark energy, critics say (Sarkar 2008, p. 269), 'may well be an artifact of an oversimplified cosmological model, rather than having physical reality'. Can DE really be an artefact of an oversimplified model? And do we have any *better,* DE-free model?

One rival DE-free model would be an inhomogeneous Lemaître–Tolman–Bondi (LTB) model (rather than the standard FLRW model, which assumes, with the **cosmological principle**, that the universe is roughly homogeneous and isotropic). If we deny homogeneity (but retain isotropy), we could assume that there are spatial variations in the distribution of matter in the universe, and that we might be occupying an underdense or 'void' region of the universe (a 'Hubble bubble'), which is expanding at a faster rate than the average. Thus, the argument goes, our inference about DE may well be flawed because based on a flawed model, i.e. by assuming a homogeneous FLRW model. A rival LTB model, it is argued (Sarkar 2008), can fit data about the fluctuations in the CMB responsible for large-scale structure (see Chapter 2), and can also account for the main source of evidence for DE, namely the use of supernova Ia data as standard candles, with an important caveat though.

Supernova Ia data, which typically are the main evidence for an *accelerating* expansion of the universe (which is in turn explained by appealing to DE), are now interpreted *without assuming acceleration.* For example, DE critics argue, light travelling through an inhomogeneous universe does not 'see' the Hubble expansion, and we make inferences about an accelerating expansion using effectively redshifts and light intensity, neither of which can track the matter density or eventual inhomogeneities of the universe through which light travels: 'could the acceleration of the universe be just a trick of light, a misinterpretation that arises due to the oversimplification of the real, inhomogeneous universe inherent in the FRW [FLRW] model?' (Enqvist 2008, p. 453). However, it should be noted that most cosmologists find LTB models unappealing, because of the need to place ourselves very close to the centre of an atypical spherical anomaly: having us occupy a 'special' position (a 'Hubble bubble') in the universe violates the Copernican principle.

Whatever the intrinsic merit of an alternative, inhomogeneous LTB model of the universe might be, one may legitimately retort against DE critics that the charge of being ad hoc seems to affect, after all, the interpretation of supernova Ia data here (as implying no acceleration), no less than it affects postulating a non-zero vacuum energy density to explain the same data as those for an accelerating expansion of the universe.

What if, instead of modifying FLRW models, we try to modify GR itself to avoid DE? So far, we do not have convincing alternatives to GR. Some physicists appeal to **string theory** to speculate that there might be many vacua with very many different values of vacuum energy, and again we might just happen to occupy one with a tiny positive energy density. Along similar lines, 'dark gravity' is also invoked to explain the accelerated expansion of the universe without DE, but in terms of a modified GR with implications for gravity. But it is fair to say that 'at the theoretical level, there is as yet no serious challenger to ΛCDM' (Durrer and Maartens 2008, p. 328).

Shifting to rivals to DM, as mentioned above, the prominent alternative candidate is MOND (modified Newtonian dynamics), first proposed by Milgrom (1983), and in its relativistic form by Bekenstein (2010). As mentioned above, MOND was introduced to explain the flat rotation curves of galaxies without the need to resort to halos of DM, but by tweaking instead Newton's second law. MOND-supporters appeal to arguments from simplicity and mathematical elegance to assert that 'for disk galaxies MOND is more economical, and more falsifiable, than the DM paradigm' (Bekenstein 2010, p. 5). Moreover, Bekenstein's work has made it possible to extend the applicability of MOND to other phenomena that were previously regarded as only explicable within the ΛCDM model, i.e. the spatial distribution of galaxies and fluctuations in the CMB. It is interesting here that appeal should be made again to Popper's falsifiability and even to the simplicity of MOND as an argument for preferring MOND over DM, which brings us back to our philosophical topic for this chapter. Is theory choice really underdetermined in current cosmology? Was Kuhn right in claiming that neither simplicity, nor accuracy or any of the other criteria involved in theory choice, will ever be sufficient to determine the rationality of theory choice?

Two considerations are worth noting in this context. First, the empirical equivalence premise in the underdetermination argument relies on the idea that two theories may have the same empirical consequences. So given an anomalous phenomenon (say, galaxy flat rotation curves) DM and MOND can be said to be empirically equivalent because they can both entail this phenomenon. Or, given the accelerating expansion as a phenomenon, both DE and inhomogeneous LTB models can be said to be empirically equivalent, because the accelerating expansion of the universe follows from either. But obviously there is much more to the choice between two theories than just considerations of their ability to *imply the same piece of empirical evidence*. Philosophers of science have sometimes appealed to the notion of **empirical support** as a more promising way of thinking about theory choice (Laudan and Leplin 1991). A model, say ΛCDM, is empirically supported not just when there is *direct experimental evidence* for some of its main theoretical assumptions (DE and DM), but when the model is integrated/embedded into a broader theoretical framework (i.e. GR). In this way, the model in question (e.g. ΛCDM) can receive *indirect empirical support* from any other piece of evidence which, although not a direct consequence of the model itself, is nonetheless a consequence of the broader theoretical framework in which the theory is embedded. The rationale for switching to this way of thinking about empirical support is twofold. First, as Laudan and Leplin (1993) wittily point out, having direct empirical evidence for a hypothesis or theory may not per se be sufficient to establish the hypothesis or theory as true: a televangelist that recommends reading scriptures as evidence for inducing puberty in young males and cites as evidence a sample of the male population in his town would not be regarded as having established the validity of his hypothesis.

Second, and most importantly, scientists' reluctance to modify Newtonian dynamics or to amend GR (by rejecting FLRW models for example) reflects more than just good sense, or 'entrenchment'. There are very good reasons for holding onto such theories given the extensive range of empirical evidence for them. Thus, one might argue that although MOND is indeed an elegant and simple mathematical alternative to DM, there are reasons for resisting modifications of Newtonian dynamics in general, given the success of Newtonian dynamics over centuries in accounting for a variety of phenomena (from celestial to terrestrial mechanics). Although none of the phenomena from terrestrial mechanics (e.g. harmonic oscillator, pendulum) are of course directly relevant to galaxy flat rotation curves, one might legitimately appeal to the success of Newtonian dynamics across this wide-ranging spectrum of phenomena as an argument for Newtonian dynamics being well supported by evidence and not being in need of ad hoc modifications to account for recalcitrant pieces of evidence in cosmology.

Not surprisingly, the philosophers' notion of empirical support chimes with and complements the physicists' multiprobe methodology in the search for DE in large galaxy surveys. Integrating multiple probes presents of course important challenges, especially when it comes to calibration, cross-checks, and the perspectival nature of the data set coming from different methods. But it also shows how methodologically important and heuristically fruitful the multiprobe procedure may be to dissipating the threat of empirical equivalence, which – as we have seen – looms in current debates about DE and DM. But this is a story for some other time.

Chapter summary

- Dark energy and dark matter have been postulated to explain two anomalous phenomena (i.e. the accelerating expansion of the universe, and galaxies' flat rotation curves). But rival explanations for these two phenomena are also possible without appealing to DE and DM.

- This is an example of what philosophers call the problem of underdetermination of theory by evidence. A piece of negative (or anomalous) evidence can be the sign that either a new auxiliary hypothesis has to be introduced or that the main theoretical assumptions need to be modified.

- The underdetermination argument proceeds from the premise of empirical equivalence between two theories to the conclusion that the rationality of theory choice is underdetermined by evidence.

- Appeals to good sense, entrenchment, or sociological considerations, do not solve or mitigate the problem of underdetermination of theory by evidence.

- The adoption of the DM plus DE model as standard took some time to be established. Strong evidence for a DE-dominated universe was available around 1990 but initially met with scepticism, based in part on the (continuing) difficulty in understanding physically how the vacuum density could be non-zero at a small level.

- But the evidence for an accelerating expansion from Type Ia supernovae in 1998 accomplished an almost instant adoption of the new standard model. These results in themselves could have been (and were) challenged, but the observational consistency with other lines of argument was sufficient to trigger a paradigm shift.

- Nevertheless, there is a growing interest in asking whether the inferred existence of DM and DE as physical substances is really correct. This conclusion rests in particular on assuming that the law of gravity as measured locally still applies on the scale of the universe.

- Rivals to DE appeal to inhomogeneous LTB (Lemaître–Tolman–Bondi) models, or to modified GR (general relativity). The first implies a violation of the Copernican principle; the second involves appeal to string theory, and no unique and well-motivated alternative to GR is currently available.

- The main rival to DM is MOND (modified Newtonian dynamics). Despite the simplicity and mathematical elegance of MOND, it has not won general consensus, because it involves a violation of Newtonian dynamics that many find unattractive.

- Perhaps a solution to the problem of underdetermination consists in introducing a notion of empirical support, which can resolve prima facie empirical equivalence between rival theories, by looking at the broader theoretical framework within which each theory is embedded, and from which it can receive indirect empirical support.

50   *Michela Massimi and John Peacock*

Study questions

1 Can you explain in your own words what it means to say that evidence underdetermines theory choice?
2 Why does the underdetermination argument pose a threat to scientific realism?
3 How did the philosopher of science Thomas Kuhn portray the process that leads scientists to abandon an old paradigm and to embrace a new one? Are there any objective criteria in theory choice?
4 What is the difference between an open and closed universe, and how does this degree of spacetime curvature influence the expansion of the universe?
5 What are WIMPs, and how might they be detected?
6 What was the role of supernovae in establishing the fact that the universe is expanding at an accelerating rate?
7 What is the uncertainty principle? Explain why it requires that the vacuum density cannot be zero.
8 Is theory choice in contemporary cosmology underdetermined by evidence? Discuss the problems and prospects of rivals to both dark energy and dark matter.

Note

1 In the 1820s, the astronomer Friedrich Wilhelm Bessel hypothesized a possible departure from Newton's inverse-square law of gravity to account for the anomalous perihelion of Uranus, due to specific gravity varying from one body to another. But the hypothesis was experimentally falsified and abandoned by the 1840s.

Introductory further reading

Duhem, P. (1906/1991) *The Aim and Structure of Physical Theory*, Princeton: Princeton University Press. (This is the classic book where the problem of underdetermination was expounded for the first time.)
Feyerabend, P. (1975) *Against Method: Outline of an Anarchist Theory of Knowledge*, London: New Left Books. (Another must read for anyone with an interest in scientific methodology, or better lack thereof!)
Kuhn, T. S. (1962/1996) *The Structure of Scientific Revolutions*, 3rd edn, Chicago: University of Chicago Press. (A cult book that has shaped and changed the course of philosophy of science in the past half century.)
Kuhn, T. S. (1977) 'Objectivity, value judgment, and theory choice', in T. S. Kuhn, *The Essential Tension*, Chicago: University of Chicago Press. (Excellent collection of essays by Kuhn. This chapter in particular discusses the five aforementioned criteria for theory choice.)
Kukla, A. (1996) 'Does every theory have empirically equivalent rivals?', *Erkenntnis* 44: 137–66. (This article presents the argument from empirical equivalence to underdetermnation and assesses its credentials.)

Lahav, O. and Massimi, M. (2014) 'Dark energy, paradigm shifts, and the role of evidence', *Astronomy & Geophysics* 55: 3.13–3.15. (Very short introduction to the underdetermination problem in the context of contemporary research on dark energy.)

Laudan, L. and Leplin, J. (1991) 'Empirical equivalence and underdetermination', *Journal of Philosophy* 88: 449–72. (This is the article that put forward the notion of empirical support as a way of breaking the empirical equivalence premise.)

van Fraassen, B. (1980) *The Scientific Image*, Oxford: Clarendon Press. (This book is a landmark in contemporary philosophy of science. It is a manifesto of a prominent anti-realist view, called constructive empiricism.)

Advanced further reading

Bekenstein, J. D. (2010) 'Alternatives to dark matter: modified gravity as an alternative to dark matter', ArXiv e-prints 1001.3876.

Durrer, R. and Maartens, R. (2008) 'Dark energy and dark gravity: theory overview', *General Relativity and Gravitation* 40: 301–28.

Enqvist, K. (2008) 'Lemaitre–Tolman–Bondi model and accelerating expansion', *General Relativity and Gravitation* 40: 1–16.

Jain, B. and Khoury, J. (2010) 'Cosmological tests of gravity', ArXiv e-prints 1004.3294

Milgrom, M. (1983) 'A modification of the Newtonian dynamics: implications for galaxy systems', *Astrophysical Journal* 270: 384–9.

Quine, W. V. O. (1951) 'Two dogmas of empiricism', *Philosophical Review* 60: 20–43. (An all-time classic on the problem of underdetermination. It builds on Duhem's pioneering work and further develops the thesis. Very advanced reading.)

Sarkar, S. (2008) 'Is the evidence for dark energy secure?', *General Relativity and Gravitation* 40: 269–84.

Internet resource

Dark Energy Survey (n.d.) [website], www.darkenergysurvey.org (accessed 2 June 2014). (This is the official site of one of the current largest dark energy survey by mapping 200 million galaxies by 2018 by integrating four different probes.)

4 The anthropic principle and multiverse cosmology

John Peacock and Alasdair Richmond

Introduction: being stardust

Our night skies contain stars in different stages of development – newly formed bright stars, swollen red giants and dense stellar remnants like neutron stars. Why such diversity? We observe this range of stars because we are chemically complex beings who require several different elements in order to survive – from simple, abundant elements like hydrogen through to heavier, rarer elements like iron and sodium. Nucleosynthesis (the fusion of nucleons to form atoms) almost certainly began within 3 minutes of the Big Bang and produced the hydrogen and helium that formed the first stars. Heavier elements usually form only through *stellar* nucleosynthesis, i.e. nuclear fusion inside stars, and have to be distributed before they can form complex structures and (thereby) life. Heavier elements only get scattered across space when stars grow old and explode as supernovae. We are literally stardust. Before we could evolve, supernovae had to occur. Hence our night sky contains the remnants of old stars – times containing only young stars boasted few observers. It's not surprising complex creatures like us don't live three minutes after the Big Bang, when only hydrogen and helium existed in quantity. Looking at the kinds of observers we are and the elements that compose us supports deductions about the stars we will observe and when in the universe's history we will live. These are anthropic effects.

The anthropic principle

Anthropic reasoning reflects the important philosophical idea that good explanations should make whatever you're trying to explain more probable or typical. You should expect, all else being equal, to be in a probable or typical location for creatures like yourself. We usually favour explanations that make our location unexceptional rather than exceptional – it is not an explanatory virtue to make something less probable.

The anthropic principle is an umbrella name for a range of different observations about how the sort of observers we are reflects our place in the physical world. The term was coined by physicist Brandon Carter and first appeared in print in Carter (1974). Despite subsequent widespread use by scientists and philosophers, the anthropic principle has been defined independently in different, often incompatible ways. Carter's key idea reflects the complex and subtle interrelations between the kinds of observers we are and the physical conditions we observe. Many fortuitous contingencies (e.g. the presence of carbon, the three-dimensionality of macroscopic space, electromagnetic forces being 10^{40} times more powerful than gravitational forces, etc.) appear necessary for observers like us to evolve.

For many centuries, science assumed our place in the universe was uniquely privileged. The Ptolemaic astronomy that prevailed until the sixteenth century placed the Earth (and hence humanity) at the centre of the universe, and the planets and stars in concentric orbits around us. However, the heliocentric (sun-centred) astronomy associated primarily with Nicolaus Copernicus dethroned us from a privileged centre and, coupled with discoveries in geology, suggested the universe extends far further in space and time than had hitherto been thought. Just as the Earth is a tiny fraction of the universe's spatial extent, so humanity's recorded history is a tiny fraction of the universe's history. Charles Darwin's discovery of evolution by **natural selection** suggested human beings could fruitfully be considered as one more product of undirected, non-intentional processes. Natural selection lets us explain how complex living things (even life) can arise, without invoking external oversight or Design.

After this apparent dethroning of humanity, one might go to the opposite extreme and conclude there is nothing remarkable about our location in space and time at all. However, excessive insistence on our typicality is also misleading, since human beings are not scattered haphazardly throughout space and time. Only the Earth in the solar system offers just the right temperature conditions for carbon-based life – orbiting in the so-called 'Goldilocks zone': neither too hot nor too cold but just right. Because carbon is tetravalent (i.e. has four valency opportunities in its outermost electron-shell), it can form long-chain molecules. Carbon is great for forming complicated chemical structures using many different elements and hence is the best element known for building life. Life needs carbon chemistry; carbon chemistry needs a narrow range of temperatures, and that range is found only on Earth. Barring one, the solar system's many bodies are very hostile to life, being (e.g.) too hot, too cold, too volcanic, riddled with radiation, having unbreathable atmospheres, etc. So unsurprisingly, the solar system is mostly dead. Of all the bodies in the solar system, only one bears the right conditions for life, and (unsurprisingly) that one is Earth.

Anthropic arguments seek to balance excessive anthropocentrism and excessive insistence on human typicality: the conditions we observe may be typical for observers but atypical of the universe as a whole. We are physically based observers and can only survive (and evolve) in very specific physical circumstances – we require an environment where carbon can form complex chain molecules, where water is readily available in liquid form and where oxygen can be breathed. We require a planetary environment in which to live, and specifically one which is not subject to extremes of temperature, pressure and radiation. Hence we need to live on a planet with a breathable atmosphere and a stable orbit about its parent star. We require different elements, ranging from the lightest (i.e. hydrogen) through to heavier elements like iron and selenium. Furthermore, it seems observers like us can only survive in universes where space is three-dimensional (at least at the scale of everyday objects). Our world has three (macroscopic) mutually perpendicular, spatial axes – running left–right, up–down and forward–back. You don't live in a two-dimensional plane or in a space with four or more dimensions. Why? In less than three dimensions, nerves can't run through cells without crossing one another and nervous systems like ours cannot exist. However, in four (or more) dimensions, it's very hard to enclose volumes, hence cells and complex organs can't function.

Many apparently incidental features of the universe have something in common: they cannot differ from what we observe and still have observers around to notice them. The physical conditions we observe appear 'fine-tuned' into the narrow band that permits life. Does fine-tuning show the universe was designed or generated so that life had to evolve in it? While some anthropically inspired arguments claim life is the reason (or goal) which the universe exists to serve, such arguments may go rather beyond what anthropic effects actually suggest.

Anthropic arguments begin by noting that the conditions necessary for context-sensitive observers set restrictions on the sorts of conditions such observers will probably find themselves observing. 'Anthropic' comes from the Greek *anthropos*, which literally means 'Man', but anthropic reasoning makes no special reference to humans in general, or male humans in particular. Any physical observers can use anthropic reasoning: 'The same self-selection principle would be applicable by any extra-terrestrial civilisation that may exist' (Carter 1983, p. 348). Different kinds of observers would find the conditions necessary for their evolution constraining their observations too. Carbon-based observers like us are more likely to find ourselves in conditions suitable for carbon-based life. If you were a sulphur-based observer, expect to have evolved in conditions amenable to the evolution of sulphur-based observers. (Likewise, if you're made of high-energy plasma, expect to find yourself in plasma-friendly conditions – e.g. inside a star's hot interior.) Likewise, anthropic reasoning need not imply any (Design or other) intentional explanation for our existence. Both anthropic and natural selection explanations explain features that suggest Design but in non-Design terms. Anthropic reasoning assumes life is highly context-sensitive and requires a narrow range of physical conditions. Postulating an intelligent Designer outside the physical universe assumes intelligence can transcend our physical environment. So arguing from fine-tuning to Design risks arguing from fine-tuning to the conclusion that consciousness does not require fine-tuning at all.

Forms of the anthropic principle

Closest to Carter's original proposal is the **weak anthropic principle** (WAP): 'What we can expect to observe must be restricted by the conditions necessary for our presence as observers' (Carter 1974, p. 291). Any observers who require a delicate range of conditions for their sustenance will almost certainly only evolve where those conditions are met. Typical observers should inhabit amenable surroundings. If you're thinking 'But I'm a unique snowflake of a person', and bridling at being described as typical, here are some tests:

- Are you based on silicon, sulphur or selenium?
- Are you a cloud of high-temperature plasma?
- Are you living inside a supernova?
- Did you grow up on a neutron star?

Presumably not. While you are a unique and irreplaceable human being, it does not follow that you are unique in *absolutely every way*. We're all unique in various ways, but we're also fairly typical in various ways. Context-sensitive observers will more likely find themselves evolving in, and hence observing, areas of spacetime which are hospitable to them but possibly atypical of the universe at large. Hence, WAP suggests we should beware of extrapolating too hastily from the conditions we observe in our spatiotemporal neighbourhood to conditions in the universe as a whole. Thus, anthropic reasoning seems to counterbalance the Copernican principle, which counsels us to view ourselves and our environment as being as typical as possible. However, any tension between anthropic and Copernican thinking is more apparent than real. Another test: observers will probably live in (comparatively rare) planetary environments and not in (very common) interstellar or intergalactic space. You aren't reading this floating unprotected in interstellar space, for all that interstellar space is vastly bigger than the Earth. Interstellar space is much more 'typical' of conditions in the universe as a whole – but interstellar conditions are deeply inimical to life and it's not surprising you neither evolved there nor reside there.

According to one popular misreading, WAP says (e.g.) 'Observers must have evolved where they have evolved', as though WAP was a mere tautology like 'All swans are swans'. As a result, it's often thought WAP must be devoid of any practical or scientific implications. However, WAP does *not* say 'You evolved where you evolved', which would be tautologous, but: 'You are far more likely to have evolved in conditions suitable for your evolution'. While it is overwhelmingly more probable that you evolved in conditions suitable for your evolution, it is conceivable that it was not so. In a big enough universe (or universe-ensemble), some very odd observers may exist, who arose in conditions where their evolution would be very unlikely. However, you should not expect to find yourself among such unusual observers. An example: if we assume consciousness is purely material or generated by material structures, then it's conceivable (albeit *astronomically* unlikely) that minds like ours could spring into existence fully formed through pure happenstance. Maybe lightning struck some chemicals in a swamp and triggered spontaneous cellular activity that issued in me, complete with false memories of a life I never had. This non-evolutionary 'swamp person' story 'explains' my physical and mental make-up. (In a sufficiently big universe, or universe-ensemble, with sufficient variation in conditions, the generation of swamp-people somewhere in space and time will be a certainty.) However, it's a poor explanation that makes me so bizarrely atypical. I won't accept the 'swamp man' story unless I find exceptionally powerful evidence in its favour: if I think most conscious observers arise through evolutionary processes and I've no reason to regard myself as an exception to this generalization, then I should believe I too evolved.

Some scientists and philosophers (not least Brandon Carter) took this 'tautology' criticism as a challenge and proposed ways to derive empirical predictions from WAP. Carter (1983) considers the number of crucial steps that are necessary for advanced life forms to evolve, noting that the time it took intelligent life to evolve on Earth (*c.* 3.5 billion years) is of the same order of magnitude as the age of the Earth (*c.* 4.5 billion years) and the likely time remaining before the sun burns out (again *c.* 4.5 billion years). Why does the time the Earth has been in existence resemble the time it took observers like us to evolve? In Carter's (1983) terms, life had to take a number of 'crucial steps' while evolving intelligent observers, e.g. generating multicellular from unicellular life. Many of these steps might have taken millions of years. Carter says the apparent similarity between the Earth's age and the history of Earthly life is explicable in anthropic terms if intelligent life typically takes *longer* to evolve than the life-sustaining period of its parent star. Thus, most life forms will take only a few crucial steps towards intelligence before their parent stars die, and so make further evolution impossible nearby. Most potentially life-supporting stars do not support life long enough to let intelligence evolve. So, Carter (1983) predicts, even if extraterrestrial *life* is common, extraterrestrial *intelligence* is rare. Carter's formula explains the so-called 'Great Silence' from alien life forms (as in **Fermi's paradox**): if the Earth is a typical abode of life, and many extraterrestrials exist, where are they? Perhaps Earth is a specially maintained 'zoo' surrounded by aliens who observe us undetectably. A 'cosmic zoo' hypothesis is hard to falsify but more importantly, it makes us very atypical life forms, and is thus counter-anthropic. On this hypothesis, typical observers don't live in zoos.

The **strong anthropic principle** (SAP) generalizes WAP and says the presence of observers suggests the universe is amenable to the evolution of such observers, thus: 'The Universe must have those properties which allow life to develop within it at some stage in its history' (Barrow and Tipler 1986, p. 21). If we assume our ancestors evolved in this universe, this universe must have boasted conditions that made such evolution possible. Thus, SAP applies WAP to the whole universe, not to any isolated subregion. SAP is often (mis)read as necessarily carrying **teleological explanation**, i.e. invoking life as the universe's goal or intended end-state, and hence claiming that the universe must (in some categorical sense) have been set up so as to produce life. Advocates and opponents of SAP alike have encouraged the idea that SAP is teleological or Design-orientated. In fact, teleological readings of SAP confuse a categorical inference with a conditional one. If I find frogs thriving in a pond, and I assume they grew there normally, I should assume the pond recently held frogspawn. Likewise, if I believe I breathe oxygen, I should believe it's likely that there has been oxygen in my environment – it does not necessarily follow that Nature has been rigged so this pond inevitably yielded frogs or that oxygen must have been present so my survival would be ensured. Given you exist, it follows your existence must be possible but it does not follow that you *must* (categorically) have existed. So the conditional WAP inference 'If we evolved hereabouts, local conditions must have been suitable for our evolution' and its generalized SAP cousin 'If we evolved in this universe, this universe must have been suitable for our evolution' seem plausibly in tune with Carter's original idea; however, less plausible is any inference that runs 'The presence of conditions suitable for life in this universe shows this universe must have been designed with such evolution in mind'. Imagine a frog in our pond reasoning: 'The presence of frog-sustaining conditions in this pond shows the laws of nature were designed for frogs'. Such seems a presumptuous frog. The Earth's diameter is roughly 12.7×10^6 m, whereas the observed universe's diameter is roughly 8.8×10^{26} m, so a pond 1 metre across occupies a vastly bigger fraction of the Earth's surface than Earth does of the observable universe.

Further extensions of anthropic reasoning include the **participatory anthropic principle** and **final anthropic principle** (PAP and FAP, respectively). PAP says observers somehow determine or create the physical properties they observe: 'Observers are necessary to bring the universe into being' (Barrow and Tipler 1986, p. 22). So, humans are not passive observers of the universe's physical order but active creators of it: we help make the natural order even as we observe it. However, while PAP often invokes quantum theory in its defence, many quantum theories do not accord consciousness any such special role.

FAP says life, once created, must thereafter endure forever: 'Intelligent information-processing must come into existence in the Universe, and, once it comes into existence, it will never die out' (ibid.). Amongst FAP's difficulties is trying to derive testable predictions that support a literally infinite future for life. FAP can make predictions, e.g. the universe must allow infinite extendibility of the material processes that sustain consciousness, but such predictions don't lend themselves readily to falsification (PAP and FAP command markedly fewer adherents than WAP or SAP).

Unnatural aspects of standard cosmology

In recent years, interest has grown in using the above ideas on anthropic observer selection to understand some of the ways in which cosmology seems puzzlingly unnatural. Naturalness is often invoked as a principle in order to see whether a physical theory may hide a deeper or simpler model. For example, the standard model of particle physics contains twenty-five numbers (if we include massive neutrinos). Can these numbers be related and/ or do some take strange values? The fundamental masses in the standard model are generally felt to be unnatural, since quantum corrections would tend to make them larger: comparable to the largest energy scale that can be imagined, which is the Planck scale of quantum gravity. This is an energy at which the fundamental idea of particles existing in an uncurved background spacetime breaks down, degenerating into a foam of quantum black holes. The characteristic energy at which this happens translates (via $E = mc^2$) to a mass of 2×10^{-8} kg. This is a very small mass by everyday standards, but huge in the world of particle physics: 10^{19} times the mass of the proton. Thus the small magnitude of the masses of elementary particles is a puzzle.

Cosmology is also unnatural to some extent. There are various coincidences of value between apparently unrelated quantities (e.g. the densities of dark and visible matter are equal to an order of magnitude; the time of matter–radiation equality is within a factor of 2 of the time of last scattering of the CMB (cosmic microwave background)). But the biggest naturalness problem is the magnitude of the dark-energy density, which is far smaller than seems at all reasonable. The measured density of dark energy is about $10^{-26.2}$ kg m^{-3}. As discussed earlier, the electromagnetic zero-point energy of the vacuum could exceed this figure unless we cut off the contribution from high-frequency radiation. In practice, this cut-off must be performed at a wavelength of 0.5 mm, which makes no sense at all. The corresponding photons are less energetic than the most energetic photons produced in the LHC (Large Hadron Collider) by about a factor of 10^{15}; so even if we assume that some new physics is just around the corner at CERN, the characteristic energy of the vacuum is unnaturally low. A more dramatic way of emphasizing the same point is to go to the extreme of cutting off at the energy scale of quantum gravity, the Planck scale. In that case, the vacuum density would be over-predicted by about 120 powers of 10. Either way, there is a major puzzle here.

In considering such naturalness arguments, we are clearly taking a probabilistic view: a low dark-energy density seems 'unlikely', requiring an unusual cancellation. This is implicitly a Bayesian approach – i.e. treating the degree of belief in a theory as a probability. The Bayesian view of statistics can be controversial, and things are more clear-cut when we know that an ensemble of outcomes exists, so that probability can be defined simply via relative frequency. Remarkably, this is very much the case in modern cosmology, where the preferred models inevitably create a **multiverse** of causally disconnected bubbles, each of which can display different forms of the 'laws of physics'. Given such an ensemble, it is possible to go one step further and ask about how the different physics in the different bubbles can influence the probability of observers arising. In this way, issues such as the strange value of the measured dark energy density can potentially be understood as arising from observer selection out of the ensemble.

Multiverses seem to run afoul of **Ockham's razor**, or the principle of ontological parsimony. However, Ockham's razor only cautions against multiplying entities beyond necessity, where multiverse theories have unique explanatory potential. Secondly, Ockham's razor may only counsel *qualitative* economy (i.e. economy over the number of different kinds of things) and not *quantitative* economy (i.e. economy over the number of similar things postulated). Certainly, this mode of reasoning is increasingly seen as an attractive mode of cosmological explanation, for reasons we now articulate.

The inflationary multiverse

The concept of **inflationary cosmology** was mainly developed in the early 1980s, although the essential idea first arose in a visionary 1965 paper by the Soviet cosmologist E. B. Gliner. The desire was to remove the need to supply arbitrary initial conditions for the Big Bang model: what started the expansion at $t = 0$? What happened before this initial singularity? Most especially, how was the early universe able to start in such a symmetric and uniform state? This last problem is especially challenging, although less obvious at first sight; it is known as the horizon problem. To see the difficulty, imagine that two observers within the current universe wish to exchange information about their local conditions (the mass density, the CMB temperature, etc.). This takes time, since light signals need to be exchanged: a billion years for points one billion light years apart. But once the signals have been exchanged, the observers will find that they experience very much the same conditions, with CMB temperatures equal to 1 part in 100,000. Clearly there must have been a previous episode of **causal contact** in order to set this uniform temperature, and it might be thought that this would be easy to arrange, since points now separated by a billion light years were once only (say) 1 centimetre apart. But the solution of the Friedmann equation shows that the universe expanded very rapidly near the Big Bang, so that causal contact only occurs progressively. Today, when we observe the CMB, we see radiation that has been travelling since near the start of the Big Bang, so we are looking out to a distance of order 10^{10} light years. We can see to this **horizon distance** in two opposite directions, which thus have twice the separation – and therefore cannot yet have come into causal contact with each other. Nevertheless, we can see that they have the same temperature: so causal contact must have occurred, even though it is apparently impossible in the framework of the hot Big Bang expansion.

A more detailed analysis reveals that the solution to the horizon problem requires that the expansion of the universe should be accelerating at early times, rather than the strong deceleration expected in the standard Big Bang. Gliner's initial insight was that this could happen if the equation of the state of the universe changed at early times: being dominated by vacuum energy (in effect an extremely large cosmological constant), which later decays into radiation. In this case, the early expansion of the universe would be exponential in form – i.e. without a singularity even in the infinite past. But what is the mechanism for changing the vacuum density? This was invented by Peter Higgs in 1964. In order to explain the masses of elementary particles (particularly why the W and Z particles that carry the weak nuclear force were not massless), he postulated that the universe was filled with a **scalar field**, ϕ, and moreover that this field generated an energy density as a function of the field value, $V(\phi)$. The detection of the Higgs boson in 2013 tells us not only that the field exists, but that it can change with time: the Higgs particle corresponds to small oscillations about the minimum in $V(\phi)$. This gives the desired mechanism: $V(\phi)$ in effect functions as a changeable energy density of the vacuum. In practice, we cannot explain an inflationary start to the universe using the Higgs field, but it is assumed that another scalar field (the inflaton) exists and can have the required properties.

In this way, Guth, Linde and other pioneers explained how the universe could begin without a Big Bang (or, at least, without the Big Bang being where we thought – this time is now simply the point at which **inflation** ended, where the density from the inflaton ceased to dominate the total). The theory also explains how the universe can be so large and uniform: a tiny patch of subnuclear scale is inflated during the inflationary period so that it becomes a bubble of scale very much greater than the presently visible universe. One should picture a watermelon as the inflated bubble, with one of the black seeds representing the sphere of radius roughly 10^{10} light years, which is all that we can observe. Inflation therefore explicitly predicts that there is much more to the universe than we can observe. In space, it continues exponentially far beyond the maximum scales we can observe. In time, it is unclear how long the universe has existed. A Big Bang singularity can predate the start of inflation, but once there has been sufficient expansion for vacuum-dominated expansion to set in, things settle down to very nearly exponential expansion – which is hard to distinguish from a state that has persisted forever. Thus inflation explains the puzzles about the apparent Big Bang singularity (which is an illusion), but by making it very hard to learn anything about any true ultimate Big Bang.

Unexpectedly, it became clear by 1982 that inflation also explained the origin of structure in the universe, via quantum fluctuations in the early stages of inflation when our current universe was of subnuclear scale. In retrospect, this period in the early 1980s therefore stands out as one of the most stunning eras of progress in physics – matched only by the revolution of quantum mechanics in the early 1920s. At a stroke, a new view of cosmology sprang into being, which in principle offered answers to all the puzzles about how the initial conditions of our current universe were set. This is an astonishing and ambitious vision, but how can it be tested? The key point is that quantum fluctuations should exist in all fields, and therefore inflation predicted not merely fluctuations in density, but a corresponding set of fluctuating primordial gravitational waves. These would fill the universe in the same way as the photons of the microwave background radiation: arriving almost uniformly from all directions, and traceable to a 'last scattering surface' – but since gravitational radiation is much more weakly interacting than electromagnetic radiation, the gravitational waves would have interacted much earlier in time: back during the era of inflation in which they were generated.

For decades, detecting these ultimate messengers of the early universe seemed a rather ambitious goal. But astonishingly, on 17 March 2014, the BICEP2 experiment claimed that they had been seen. These relic gravitational waves cannot be seen directly, but via the CMB: they originate 'behind' the CMB's surface of last scattering, and perturb the primordial plasma that exists at this time as they pass through it. The result is to add a characteristic pattern of polarization into the CMB, and it is this polarization signal that was detected, using a telescope observing from the USA's base at the South Pole. So in what sense have the gravitational waves been 'detected'? Experiments on Earth have sought these waves for decades, and most are in the form of an interferometer, where lasers measure the separation between two freely hanging mirrors, looking for a change in separation as a gravitational wave passes through. So is there any real difference between a detection in a local experiment and a detection via the CMB, even though in the latter case we cannot touch the matter that the gravitational waves cause to move? A line does tend to be drawn between 'experimental' science such as laboratory physics and 'observational' science, of which astronomy is the archetype. The distinction is that astronomy has to function with the universe as its laboratory, and experiments designed by nature, rather than under the control of the experimenter. Astronomers tend to be less concerned by the distinction: if an experiment works, who cares who designed it? Part of the attraction of the subject for researchers is indeed the challenge of overcoming natural experiments that yield less information than would be desirable.

This purely observational nature of astronomy becomes strongly apparent when considering a discovery as potentially important as the BICEP2 experiment. Science requires replication and cross-checking, and that is especially true with a discovery of such potential importance. But the result cannot be checked with an independent technique, so other experimenters will seek to measure the same CMB polarization signature. Initially, a focus will probably even be given to observing the same part of the sky, to verify that different telescopes see the same thing. In addition, it will be necessary to understand in more detail the issue of foregrounds: are we sure that the claimed signal is truly cosmological, and not produced by emission from within our own Milky Way that is larger than expected? At the time of writing, evidence has recently emerged that the level of such foregrounds is expected to be larger than estimated by the BICEP2 team, and potentially consistent with their signal. At present, it is therefore not possible to make any definitive claims that primordial gravitational waves have been detected – but current precision of foreground estimates would permit a substantial part of the BICEP2 measurement to be truly primordial: things are fascinatingly poised.

If the BICEP2 detection is eventually confirmed, we would be able to make a number of profound claims, most notably that inflation has now shifted from being just a neat idea, to something that is considered proved. The universe would have gone through an early stage of exponential expansion, where it doubled its size about every 10^{-38} seconds; the gravitational waves would have been generated about 10^{-36} seconds before the end of inflation, when the universe was 10^{55} times smaller than at present.

Now, it is never the case that a theory can be proved true with perfect certainty. Even when many years have passed, with complete agreement between the theory and all available observations, a flaw can arise – as shown by the example of Newtonian physics, which was eventually supplanted by the relativistic approach. Thus all physical theories can only be provisional working hypotheses. In a sense, we can be happier using a framework like Newtonian physics, since we know it is an approximation that is valid in a certain regime. It is therefore a valid truth about the universe, but we are spared having to wonder whether it is the ultimate truth. In a sense, what physicists do is similar to the operation of a courtroom, where what is sought is 'proof beyond reasonable doubt': a consistent version of events that accounts for all that is known, and to which no alternative exists. In this sense, inflation will be considered proved if the BICEP2 results are verified.

A deeply significant characteristic of inflation is that it is eternal: quantum fluctuations continuously perturb the trajectory of $\phi(t)$ as it 'rolls' down the potential $V(\phi)$. Most of the time, these fluctuations cause a 'random walk' in which the scalar field meanders further from the minimum in $V(\phi)$. But every so often, it arrives by chance near the minimum and inflation comes to an end, seeding a bubble universe. This is separated by continuously inflating space from the adjacent bubble, so these members of the multiverse are causally disconnected.

Furthermore, it is easy to find ways in which the vacuum density in each bubble could be different. The modern incarnation of such physics is provided by the **landscape** of string theory. Without saying too much about what string theory is, it suffices to note that a major feature of the theory is the existence of more than 3 + 1 dimensions (an idea that goes back to Kaluza and Klein in the 1920s, and which could outlive string theory). We are creatures that do not experience the higher dimensions, but we can be influenced by them indirectly: if the universe expands in one of the higher dimensions, the radius of curvature in that dimension can affect properties such as the mass of particles. In short, the higher dimensions have to be stabilized, and the means for achieving this is the introduction of many additional scalar fields like the Higgs or inflaton, each with their own potential. The result is that there are many different points of local stability – i.e. minima in the potential function. Each of these corresponds to a different vacuum density, and the question is whether there are sufficiently many of them, given that the density must be fine-tuned to 1 part in 10^{120}, as we have seen. It was therefore an interesting step when the number of states in the string-theory vacuum was estimated as 10^{500}. Thus in principle the physics basis exists to say that different members of the inflationary multiverse could have different values of the vacuum density: very large in most cases, but occasionally very much smaller.

High values of the vacuum density suppress the gravitationally driven growth that transforms the initial small density fluctuations from inflation into astronomical structures capable of hosting life. Therefore, one can predict that the bubbles with high vacuum densities are sterile, and that the non-sterile bubbles (such as the one we inhabit) will experience a vacuum density that is high enough to be a marginally suppressing structure formation (since large values are preferred). This argument was used in 1987 by Steven Weinberg to predict that we would observe a non-zero vacuum density (at a time when there was no observational evidence for it).

This approach is a violent departure from the Copernican principle, which attempts to reach cosmological inferences by the assumption that humans are not privileged observers of the universe. Although obviously false on a local scale (a point selected at random would be most unlikely to lie so close to a star), there is no reason why our existence should depend on special features of the large-scale appearance of the universe. It is therefore a reasonable supposition that, if the universe appears isotropic (the same in all directions) about our position, it would also appear isotropic to observers in other galaxies. This is quite a powerful argument, as a universe that is isotropic about all points must also be homogeneous – i.e. with a density that is constant at a given time. So this Copernican approach is fruitful within our universe, but we now explicitly break with it when it comes to the multiverse.

Is this the end of science? We can only explain features we see in the current universe around us by postulating an infinity of other universes, mostly almost devoid of life, which we can never experience directly. This is rather like the winner of the National Lottery, who appreciates that their good fortune requires the existence of millions of losers – but whose names and addresses the winner can never know. And yet there are many cases where science makes a prediction that cannot be verified directly: we know beyond reasonable doubt that the temperature at the centre of the sun is about 15 million degrees (Celsius), even though no one will ever go there with a thermometer. We believe this to be true because it is a deduction made from a physical theory that is very thoroughly tested in regimes where we can make direct observations. If detection of primordial gravitational waves should prove inflation to be true beyond reasonable doubt, then arguably we would have to accept the multiverse as a reality in the same way.

Chapter summary

- Anthropic reasoning aims to express the links between the kind of observers that we are and the kind of physical conditions we observe.
- Anthropic reasoning concerns observers in general, and not humans (or any subgroup of humans) in particular. Any observers that require a narrow range of physical conditions to survive could apply anthropic reasoning.
- Anthropic reasoning is best captured in WAP (the weak anthropic principle), which says physical observers will not be distributed randomly in space and time but are overwhelmingly more likely to evolve in conditions amenable to their evolution.
- Sustainable forms of SAP (the strong anthropic principle) generalize WAP to the universe, and so support the existence of a 'multiverse' of many discrete physical universes, each exhibiting different physical conditions. Less sustainable versions import teleological implications and argue the universe was preprogrammed for generating life.
- PAP (the participatory anthropic principle) and FAP (final anthropic principle) risk making claims that are falsified and unfalsifiable, respectively.
- Carter's 'crucial steps' formula applies anthropic reasoning to the history of evolution. It suggests extraterrestrial life is very rare or rarely yields intelligence.
- Inflationary cosmology deals with the problems of the standard Big Bang by postulating that the earliest stages of evolution are dominated by a high effective vacuum density, generated by a Higgs-like scalar field. This causes exponential expansion, stretching out the universe, but seeding it with structure via quantum fluctuations.
- But inflation is eternal. The quantum fluctuations can push the inflaton field away from the point of minimum energy density, where inflation will end. Thus inflation ends rarely, resulting in bubbles of normal universe, separated by space that continues to inflate. These bubbles are therefore causally disconnected: their existence is a logical consequence of the theory, but they cannot be seen directly.
- The landscape of string theory predicts that each of these bubbles can contain a different vacuum density. Where the density is high (the usual case), the growth of cosmic structure is heavily suppressed. Therefore, the existence of observers requires a (rare) low vacuum density.
- This leaves us with anthropic cosmology: we are observers, and must account for this fact in considering cosmological parameters. Only in this way is it possible to understand how we currently observe the density of dark energy to be three times that of dark matter.

Study questions

1 How did Brandon Carter define the anthropic principle?
2 How do the weak and strong anthropic principles differ?

3 Can the anthropic principle be tested? If it cannot, is it a mere tautology?

4 What sorts of effects can be described as anthropic?

5 Must anthropic reasoning support teleological or Design conclusions?

6 What are Carter's conclusions about extraterrestrial life?

7 How large should the vacuum density be if there is no new physics below the energy scale of quantum gravity?

8 What is the problem of causal contact in the Big Bang, and how does inflationary cosmology solve this?

9 Why are primordial gravitational waves a test of inflation, and how might they be detected?

10 What is meant by the 'landscape of string theory'?

11 How would a much larger vacuum density affect the formation of cosmic structure?

12 Was Steven Weinberg correct in his anthropic prediction of a non-zero vacuum density?

Introductory further reading

Bostrom, N. (2002) *Anthropic Bias: Observation Selection Effects in Science and Philosophy*, London: Routledge. http://www.anthropic-principle.com/?q=book/table_of_contents (The best philosophical treatment of anthropic issues available. Chapter 3 distinguishes different kinds of anthropic reasoning clearly and in detail.)

Carter, B. (1974) 'Large number coincidences and the anthropic principle in cosmology', in M. S. Longair (ed.) *Confrontation of Cosmological Theories with Observational Data*, Dordrecht: Reidel, pp. 291–8. (The paper in which the anthropic principle was baptized. Covers a very wide range of physical effects that lend themselves to anthropic explanation.)

Leslie, J. (1989) *Universes*, London: Routledge. (Wide-ranging discussion of world-making and other anthropically relevant topics.)

Richmond, A. (2008) '*Apocalypse Now Does The Matrix*: anthropic adventures from doomsday to simulation', *THINK: Philosophy for Everyone* 17–18: 35–46. (Popular introduction to anthropic reasoning and its applications.)

Susskind, L. (2006) *The Cosmic Landscape: String Theory and the Illusion of Intelligent Design*, New York: Back Bay Books. (An introduction to the multiverse, emphasizing the possible role of string theory in allowing genuine physically distinct universes.)

Advanced further reading

Barrow, J. D. and Tipler, F. J. (1986) *The Anthropic Cosmological Principle*, Oxford: Oxford University Press. (The best single survey volume on anthropic physical effects.)

Carr, B. (2007) *Universe or Multiverse?*, Cambridge: Cambridge University Press. (A set of review articles on aspects of anthropic reasoning. A more up-to-date alternative to Barrow and Tipler 1986, shorn of some of the more extreme views found in that book.)

Carter, B. (1983) 'The anthropic principle and its implications for biological evolution', *Philosophical Transactions of the Royal Society of London A: Mathematical, Physical and Engineering Sciences*, 310: 347–63. (Applies anthropic reasoning to our evolutionary history. Derives 'crucial steps' formula for innovations in evolution, and argues intelligent extraterrestrials are rare.)

Earman, J. (1987) 'The SAP also rises: a critical examination of the anthropic principle', *American Philosophical Quarterly* 24: 307–17. (Takes a sceptical view of the utility and scientific status of anthropic arguments, and offers particular criticisms of PAP and FAP.)

Leslie, J. (ed.) (1999) *Modern Cosmology and Philosophy*, Amherst: Prometheus Books. (Extensive collection of key articles on cosmological and physical topics, many dealing directly with anthropic issues. Reprints Carter 1974.)

McMullin, E. (1993) 'Indifference principle and anthropic principle in cosmology', *Studies in History and Philosophy of Science* 24: 359–89. (Detailed survey contrasting 'Copernican' indifference or (mediocrity) conceptions and anthropic conceptions of our place in nature.)

Internet resources

Bostrom, N. (2004) *Anthropic Principle Bibliography* [book website], www.anthropic-principle.com/?q=book/bibliography (accessed 30 April 2014). (Very comprehensive bibliography to Bostrom's *Anthropic Bias*.)

Richmond, A. (2010) 'The anthropic principle', *Oxford Bibliographies* [online bibliographical resource], www.oxfordbibliographies.com/view/document/obo-9780195396 577/obo-9780195396577-0135.xml (accessed 30 April 2014). (Survey of anthropic works from a mainly philosophical perspective.)

5 Do our modern skulls house stone-age minds?

Jane Suilin Lavelle and Kenny Smith

Introduction

There is a puzzle in the philosophy of mind regarding whether we can know things which we have not had experience of. Although the debate can be traced back as far as Plato's *Meno* dialogues, it is most commonly connected to the early modern philosophers John Locke (1632–1704) and Gottfried Leibniz (1646–1716). Locke is an example of an **empiricist** thinker, expounding the view that all our knowledge comes from experience. In his *Essay concerning Human Understanding* (1690) Locke argued that the human mind starts as a blank slate, and that it is only through experience that it can be 'furnished' with knowledge. This contrasts with **nativism**, the view that we have some knowledge independently of experience. This was the position advocated by Leibniz in his *New Essays concerning Human Understanding* (*c*.1704, first published 1765).

Nowadays philosophers don't advocate extreme nativist or empiricist positions as embodied by Leibniz or Locke. Instead, the argument has shifted to the question 'How much knowledge can we have independently of experience, and what is this knowledge like?' In modern-day science, this question is reframed in terms of knowledge and cognitive abilities. We want to know the extent to which knowledge (e.g. knowledge about plants, animals or other people) is learnt from our parents and peers, and the extent to which it is genetically transmitted to us from our parents. The same goes for certain cognitive capacities, e.g. doing basic mathematical calculations, recognizing our kin or recognizing particular bodily movements as actions.

Two fields in particular have had a significant impact on how philosophers address these questions. The first is developmental psychology: through careful experimentation psychologists can reveal the cognitive capacities of very young infants. The reasoning here is straightforward: the younger the infant, the less experience she has had, and thus fewer opportunities to learn from experience. If an infant demonstrates a particular cognitive capacity before she can possibly have encountered sufficient data to develop it, then, the argument goes, that capacity can't be learned: it must be **innate**.

The second field to affect the philosophical debate about innate knowledge is evolutionary biology. This will be the focus of the current chapter. Specifically, we'll be looking at how the theory of natural selection affects philosophical accounts of how the mind[1] is structured. Our starting premise will be that the human mind is a product of natural selection; how we should understand and interpret that claim will be the source of our debate. We will start by presenting an approach known as **evolutionary psychology**. This is the hypothesis that the mind evolved as a series of 'mini-computers', each of which is a product of natural selection. These mini-computers evolved to solve specific problems which faced our ancestors, and have barely changed since the Pleistocene era (a period stretching from about 2.4 million years ago to about 10,000 years ago). If one accepts this hypothesis then one is committed to the idea that certain knowledge and cognitive capacities, namely those built into these mini-computers, are innate. Evolutionary psychologists are committed to the view that the majority of our cognitive abilities fall into this category. We will contrast the evolutionary psychology view with an alternative which emphasizes the role of non-genetic mechanisms in shaping human behaviour. In particular, we'll consider the idea that many interesting things people know and skills they have are products of social learning (learning from others), and that these evolve as they are passed from person to person.

Natural selection and adaptations

Before we can begin to address the question of how the theory of natural selection affects philosophical conceptions of the mind, we first need to be clear about what is meant by natural selection. What we present here is a broad overview of a substantial topic, so do take a look at the further readings to find out more. For our purposes, natural selection is best understood as a process of environmental filtering, where the environment filters out those organisms that are least able to survive and reproduce. In order for an organism or some part of an organism (e.g. a behaviour or physical feature) to be the product of natural selection, three conditions need to be in place:

Condition 1: There must once have been variation regarding a particular feature within a population: some members of the population had it and others did not.
Condition 2: Having the feature yields some reproductive or survival advantage to the organism.
Condition 3: The feature must be heritable. For a feature to persist in a population it needs to be passed from parent to offspring, otherwise there will be no long-term change in the population.

Features of organisms that we think are products of natural selection are known as **adaptations**. For example, beavers have a split claw on their hind feet that they use to groom their fur, and which is generally thought to be an adaptation. We assume that at some point in the species' history some beavers developed the split claw (variation in the population), and those beavers with the claw were better able to spread oil through their fur, making them more water-resistant than their peers without the split claw. The extra water-resistance meant they could spend more time in the water than the other beavers, avoiding landbound predators and collecting food for the family (the split claw yields survival and reproductive advantages). Having the claw was heritable, so the offspring of these beavers also had it, leading to a long-term change in the population.

Animals shape their environments and the selective pressures they experience

While the view that natural selection is a process of environmental filtering is a useful one, it arguably paints an unduly passive picture of natural selection, with organisms changing to fit the environment they inhabit. But this isn't always the case, as is clearly illustrated with the beavers. Beavers have lots of adaptations to suit the wetland environments they thrive in. But beavers also create wetland environments for themselves: they build dams to block rivers, thus expanding their surrounding wetland environment. Their various adaptations for living in water are selected for in part because they actively change their environment, flooding it, increasing the area that is under water and increasing the advantages that these adaptations provide. As well as increasing these selection pressures, damming reduces other selective pressures: for instance, flooding large areas where they can forage for food minimizes the time they have to spend out of the water, reducing the danger they face from predators. Beavers are a celebrated example of a phenomenon known as **niche construction**, where organisms change their environment through their own behaviour (Odling-Smee *et al.* 2003). Beavers are of course not the only animals that do this: you can no doubt think of other spectacular examples like termites building mounds, and, as we will discuss presently, humans. Niche-constructing species adapt to their environment, but they also change their environment, and therefore potentially change the pressures they adapt to.

Other routes of inheritance

Niche-constructing animals like beavers also nicely illustrate that animals can inherit more than just their genes from their parents. As well as inheriting, via their genes, various physical and behavioural adaptations, beaver kits also inherit their environment: the dam their parents have built, and the flooded land behind it. This therefore provides a type of non-genetic inheritance, sometimes called **ecological inheritance**.

Ecological inheritance is rife in humans: think of all the aspects of your environment that your parents and others shaped for you, starting with the hospital you were born in and the house that you grew up in. But as well as inheriting aspects of our environment, we also inherit knowledge and behaviours directly from our parents and others people, not via our genes but via **social learning.** The ability to learn, to modify your behaviour during your lifespan in response to your own personal interactions with your environment (e.g. through trial-and-error learning), is very common in the natural world. Social learning, learning from the behaviour of others, is also pretty common – other apes and primates do it, but also other mammals do it (e.g. rats), and birds do it, and even fish do it. But humans are undoubtedly the kings of social learning: most of the things you know and the skills you have depend to some extent on learning from others, either via explicit teaching, more informal imitation, or even more subtle social influences on behaviour. Think of all the things you know and skills that you have because you were taught by someone, or that you copied from a friend, or that you read about in a book or saw in a video on YouTube, or that you figured out for yourself just because you were hanging out with your friends in a particular context. On top of ecological inheritance, social learning provides another non-genetic mechanism for the inheritance of knowledge and behaviours, which is potentially crucial to understanding human evolution. We'll return to this idea later in the chapter.

Evolutionary psychology

The idea that some of our behaviours and physical features are inherited from our parents via our genes is uncontroversial. It's also uncontroversial that some of these **traits** are adaptations and have been preserved in our species because they allow us to flourish in particular environments. What is more controversial is how we should apply these ideas to human cognition. We will focus for the next few sections on a view known as evolutionary psychology, which is a specific hypothesis about how natural selection has shaped the brain, before turning to accounts that place much more emphasis on the role of social learning and culture.

   Evolutionary psychology is a research programme which promotes a particular way of understanding and exploring the human brain. It is organized around four central claims:

1   The human brain is a product of natural selection.
2   The human brain adapted to solve particular problems faced by our hominid ancestors during the Pleistocene era.
3   The cognitive capacities that our ancestors developed to solve problems were heritable: they could be transmitted biologically from parent to offspring.
4   The brains we have now are very similar to the brains that our ancestors evolved all those years ago.

As has already been mentioned, the first of these claims is (relatively) uncontroversial, what is in dispute is how we should develop it. Claims (2)–(4)

demonstrate the specific way in which evolutionary psychology develops claim (1). Let's go through them in turn.

If there were to be a catchy slogan for evolutionary psychology it would be that 'our modern skulls house a stone age mind'. This phrase was made popular by Lena Cosmides and John Tooby (1997), commonly acknowledged as the founders of the modern evolutionary psychology movement. They claim that the brains we have now are actually adapted to suit our ancestral environment. This is the environment in which humans as we know them now evolved, and we can place it as being within the Pleistocene Epoch. Evolutionary psychologists refer to the period during which *Homo sapiens* evolved as the **environment of evolutionary adaptation**. In the environment of evolutionary adaptation humans lived as hunter-gatherers in small groups. In the past 10,000 years, since the end of the Pleistocene, human societies have changed massively, with agriculture becoming a prominent way of life by about 5,000 years ago, to the human conditions of today where most of us live in large urban populations. But, the evolutionary psychologists observe, those 10,000 years account for only a tiny fraction of the time that hominids have roamed the earth and barely an eye-blink in evolutionary terms. For the previous 1.8 million years our existence depended largely on hunting meat and gathering vegetation to eat, and doing so successfully usually meant having to cooperate with a small number of others. Thus, the human mind evolved during this 1.8 million years to solve the kinds of problems which arose from these living conditions. Although our living conditions have changed significantly in the past 10,000 years, this is not enough time (so the argument goes) for the process of natural selection to have changed the way our minds work; consequently, we have brains that are very good at solving problems which were commonplace during the environment of evolutionary adaptation, but which are not necessarily adept at solving the problems thrown up by living in large, technology-driven urban environments where hunting and gathering are not the primary methods by which food is attained. Hence we have 'stone-age minds' in 'modern skulls'.

What kind of problems did our ancestors face? As hunter-gatherers they needed to distinguish poisonous from nutritious food. They needed to recognize and react quickly to predators like large carnivores and snakes. They needed to find appropriate places to set-up camp, away from environs that harbour diseases and possible predators. They also needed to live and work in small groups, containing kin and some non-kin. This requires being able to foster good social relations through selective cooperation, which in turn requires being able to recognize who is a good person to cooperate with. Reproductive success partially entails cooperating with kin, so you need to be able to recognize them; but it also involves keeping favour with someone who has a lot of power in the group, so you need to recognize the cues which signal dominance and change your behaviour towards those members accordingly. Conversely, you don't want to invest energy cooperating with free-riders (people who benefit from the group without contributing to it) so you need some kind of strategy for recognizing them. These and other problems recurred day after day for over a million years, forming the environmental filter, say the evolutionary psychologists, which shaped the human brain. Certain cognitive abilities, e.g. the ability to detect free-riders, are as much adaptations as the beaver's split claw. Those humans who were able to detect free-riders had a slight edge over those without this ability, and assuming this ability can be biologically transmitted to their offspring (a point we return to presently), the process of natural selection operates in just the same way as it does on the physical and behavioural attributes discussed earlier. The environment in which our ancestors lived, hunting and gathering in small groups, persisted for such a long time that there was ample opportunity for their brains to change in response to the recurrent problems of that environment. The features of the hominid brain, how it works and the behaviours it has generated, evolved during this period to better suit us to our living conditions in the environment of evolutionary adaptation.

The evolutionary psychologist's argument is beginning to come together. Humans faced distinctive recurring problems in the environment of evolutionary adaptation and those humans who survived were those who evolved reliable behaviours to address these problems. Thus the humans who survived were those who had the appropriate neural circuitry to generate the appropriate behavioural responses to the variety of problems facing the average Pleistocene human. These neural circuits persist in today's humans, even though the environmental problems we face are significantly different from those encountered by humans in the environment of evolutionary adaptation. In some cases this can lead to **maladaptation**. Maladaptations are features of organisms which exist due to the process of natural selection and thus are very well suited to the conditions of a specific stable environment. But if that environment changes and the problems which that feature evolved to respond to no longer exist, then that feature can be detrimental to the organism. For example, the trait of finding salt and fat tasty is beneficial to a Pleistocene hunter-gatherer, as it motivates her to track down calorific sources of food which will give her lots of energy to invest in rearing offspring and gathering more food. But in an environment where sources of salt and fat are rife this craving is a maladaptation, causing humans to consume far too much of these food sources resulting in health problems. The relatively new urban environment throws up survival problems which the brain has not yet had time to evolve responses to, while ancient survival mechanisms persist. Stephen Pinker (1999) puts the point nicely when he observes that we fear snakes more than driving without a seat belt. Although car accidents kill far more people each year than snakes, we have not evolved a visceral response to driving without a seat belt, but 1.8 million years in the environment of evolutionary adaptation was enough time to evolve a response to significant dangers of that time, including snakes.

Advocates of evolutionary psychology claim that the best way to study the brain, to grasp why it causes us to behave in certain ways under particular conditions, requires understanding the environmental problems the brain has evolved to solve. Researchers shouldn't just look at how the brain functions in today's environment because properly understanding the brain means looking at its evolutionary history in a particular way, namely, hypothesizing about the problems faced in the environment of evolutionary adaptation.

The mind as a series of mini-computers

The second research commitment the evolutionary psychologists hold is that the brain consists in a series of 'mini-computers', each of which evolved to respond to a particular environmental pressure, i.e. how to detect free-riders, how to recognize when someone's trying to communicate with us (rather than just moving their limbs or vocalizing unintentionally), how to recognize predators, etc.

The position that the brain consists largely in a collection of mini-computers is known as **modularity theory**, where each mini-computer is referred to as a *module*. Each mini-computer, or module, evolved to solve a particular environmental problem that faced our ancestors. There is a mini-computer which allows us to recognize faces, a mini-computer that generates a disgust reaction to certain dangerous food, a mini-computer that generates a motivational drive to seek out nutritional food, a mini-computer that allows us to detect free-riders. If one takes this view of the mind, then one sees it as composed of lots of small, specialized units, each devoted to a particular task. To borrow an analogy from Cosmides and Tooby, evolutionary psychology predicts that the brain is like a Swiss Army knife, with lots of tools each specialized to a particular job, but which aren't generally interchangeable. You can contrast this with an alternative view of the brain, which sees it as more like a chef's knife which can be used fairly effectively in a large variety of circumstances, but which isn't specialized to one particular task.

To illustrate this point, it helps to look at one of the most commonly cited studies that evolutionary psychologists see as evidence for their view. Evolutionary psychologists claim that the ability to detect free-riders is a cognitive adaptation to a problem that recurred throughout the environment of evolutionary adaptation. They argue for this claim as follows. There is a logic puzzle designed by Peter Wason in 1966 which tests whether people can tell if a particular logical rule has been broken (see Figure 5.1). The majority of participants in the first task select the cards with the circle and the chequers. Actually the correct cards to turn are the circle and the spotted card – you need to check that the spotted card does not have a circle on the other side, but it doesn't matter if the chequered card doesn't have a circle on the other side. The rule doesn't state that a chequered card must have a circle on the other side, so it is perfectly compatible with the rule if you turn that card over and find a triangle. However, the vast majority of people who take the test (including students who have taken classes in logic!) get it wrong. By contrast, success on the second test (Figure 5.2), created by Leda Cosmides twenty years after Wason's original problem, is much higher across participants, who find it easier to spot which cards need to be turned over in order to ensure the rule is kept.

You have just taken a job with a card-game manufacturer, and you're in charge of quality control. You have to ensure that the following rule has not been broken:

If a card has a circle on one side, then it is chequered on the other side.

You've been assured that each card has a pattern on one side and a shape on the other. Which card, or cards need to be turned over in order to see if the rule is broken in the case of the four cards below? Mark **only** those cards that must be turned over in order to check the rule has been followed.

Figure 5.1 Logic task (adapted from J. Strangroom, 'The Wason Selection Task', *Philosophy Experiments*, 2014, www.philosophyexperiments.com/wason/default.aspx (accessed 17 June 2014)).

Imagine you're now bored of being a quality control manager for card games, and you've taken on a position as a bouncer at a night club. You must ensure the following rule is enforced:

If a person drinks an alcoholic drink then they must be over the age of 18 years old.

Each card represents a patron of the pub. Which card, or cards need to be turned over in order to see if the rule is broken in the case of the four cards below? Again, write down only the cards that must be turned over in order to check the rule has been followed.

Figure 5.2 Social task (adapted from J. Strangroom, 'The Wason Selection Task', *Philosophy Experiments*, 2014, www.philosophyexperiments.com/wason/default. aspx (accessed 17 June 2014)).

Cosmides and Tooby maintain that the best explanation for this is that we have evolved a special mini-computer to detect free-riders in our social environment. This mini-computer starts up when we need to detect if someone has transgressed a social norm, for example, if someone is drinking alcohol they are not entitled to. But because this mini-computer is specialized to the task of detecting when people are violating social norms, it won't be activated by tasks with an identical logical structure but which are not in the social domain, e.g. tasks that require you to detect the violation of a rule governing circles and chequers. The mini-computers can only access the information relevant to their particular job. Survival in the environment of evolutionary adaptation was not affected by the ability to detect the violation of logical rules in abstract (circle-and-chequers) settings, but it seems plausible that it was affected by the ability to detect those who are violating the social standards and expectations of the group. It doesn't matter that the social norms themselves have changed since the environment of evolutionary adaptation: the point is that we can detect the violation of such norms, regardless of what the actual content of those norms might be (e.g. they might be about sharing food, or sanctioning alcohol consumption).

One of the most important arguments for the evolutionary psychologists' claim that the mind is a series of mini-computers stems from the argument that complex systems must evolve in a modular fashion. In order for complex systems to evolve it needs to be the case that they can be broken down into less complex parts, each of which evolved semi-independently of the whole. The human eye is a good example of this. First, our very distant evolutionary ancestors evolved a light sensor that could detect daily changes in light and dark. Then retinas evolved cones to detect different light wavelengths, and later rods with greater light sensitivity than cones. Many steps further on, we get to the complex system that is the human eye, with features that have gradually evolved and been added to existing light detection systems. Evolutionary pressures caused individual components of the eye to adapt, but if one component changed it wasn't necessary for all of them to change. If a component that detects colours evolves, this doesn't directly affect the existing systems that detect movement or edges, for example. And one component can be damaged but the whole organ can continue to function. For example, some people's eyes have cones with limited functionality, which affects the range of colours that they can see, but the rest of their vision functions normally.

If the brain is a product of natural selection, say the evolutionary psychologists, then we need to see it as a series of mini-computers, each of which is an adaptation to some particular cognitive problem that challenged our hunter-gatherer ancestors. Each mini-computer has access only to those other mini-computers that produce information relevant to it. In addition, natural selection can act on one mini-computer without having to change all the others. So, our ability to detect free-riders can evolve through natural selection, but this change to the brain's structure doesn't affect the mini-computers that deal with spatial cognition, predator detection, and so on. This is highly advantageous for the overall functioning of the brain, because it means that if one mini-computer breaks down the whole system does not crash. Finally, and crucially for the evolutionary psychology account, the mini-computers of the brain are heritable. They are biologically transmitted from parent to offspring just like behavioural and physical adaptations.

The role of the environment

One potential objection to the evolutionary psychology perspective is that it does not fully appreciate how important the environment is in human cognition and development. Let's assume for a moment that there is a mini-computer dedicated to picking out faces from the other visual cues in the environment, and which motivates us to pay attention to those things classified as 'faces'. As the module is heritable we expect each child to have it. But now imagine a sad case where an infant is isolated from birth and has very little contact with faces. Does evolutionary psychology predict that she will still be able to recognize certain shapes as faces when she finally encounters them? Not necessarily. The mini-computer for detecting faces might not get 'switched on' or be able to operate properly if it is in an environment where the appropriate data are scarce. Just because something is heritable does not mean that it will reliably appear in a child regardless of environmental conditions. An analogy might help here: the biological trait of growing milk teeth is heritable and not learned from our parents. But a child in a malnourished environment might not develop milk teeth. This does not mean she has not inherited that biological feature, or that developing milk teeth is not a trait which has evolved through natural selection, but rather that the environment that she is currently in does not allow that trait to manifest itself. The same, argues the evolutionary psychologist, can happen to cognitive modules: they require certain environmental input to be activated. However, the environment isn't necessarily limited to triggering innate knowledge: in the next few sections we'll see how non-genetic 'environmental' routes of transmission can have important consequences for human behaviour and human evolution.

Social learning and cumulative culture

We've already mentioned how humans have a whole set of knowledge and behaviours that are transmitted by social learning rather than the genes: we acquire knowledge and skills by learning them from other people. The catch-all term for this socially learned repertoire is **culture**, which in its technical use just means any system of knowledge or behaviour which is transmitted through teaching, imitation, or other kinds of social learning. Your culture includes the clothes you wear, the technologies you use, the religious beliefs and social customs of your population, and the language you speak.

Other animals have culture too, because they do social learning. The cultures of non-human animals are very simple: they look as if one smart animal comes up with an innovative way of doing something, and this behaviour spreads through the population via social learning. Because of this, each population gradually develops its own idiosyncratic collection of these simple behaviours – their own culture.

The knowledge and behaviours that make up human culture don't work like this: rather than being a collection of simple individual components, the products of human culture are enormously complex. Think of how complex a bicycle is, or a car, or a computer, or even your clothes with all the different fabrics, stitches, buttons, and zips. Or think about how sophisticated the legal and political system is in your country, and how it got to be that way. These complex objects weren't invented by one smart individual. They represent the gradual accumulation of modifications over hundreds and thousands of years. People take an existing object or behaviour, change (and probably improve) its design a bit, then pass on that modified object. This process, where one generation builds on the knowledge they inherit from a previous generation, is called **cumulative culture**, and it produces enormously intricate, well-designed objects. So at least some of the adaptive behaviours and artefacts that humans possess aren't products of biological evolution – they are the products of cumulative culture.

Culture influences biological evolution in humans

Cast your mind back to the case of the beavers and their dams. Humans do exactly the same kind of sculpting and shaping of their environment, but on a massive scale. Unlike beavers, the majority of the things we do to shape our environment – wearing clothes, building shelter, growing crops and keeping animals for food, living in large, complex social groups – are not instinctive behaviours, but socially learned: they are part of culture, and you learn how to do these things from the people around you. However, although the way we inherit these behaviours is different (social learning, rather than via the genes), the modifications we humans make to our environment massively change the selective pressure acting on us, in the same way as beavers and their dams. Our ability to insulate ourselves from hostile environments with clothing and housing has allowed us to spread right across the planet, and inhabit environments – like the high plains of the Andes, or the Arctic Circle – which would otherwise be uninhabitable.

As with the beavers, as well as insulating ourselves from selective pressures coming from the environment, our cultural practices have also set up new selective pressures. One of the most famous cases is the evolution of **lactase persistence**. Most mammals, including the majority of humans, lose the ability to digest lactose, the main carbohydrate in milk, once they are weaned: there's simply no need to carry on producing lactase, the enzyme that the body uses to break down lactose, once you have stopped drinking your mother's milk. But a minority of the world's human population (about 30 per cent of people, mainly located in Northern Europe and North Africa) continue to produce lactase long after weaning, throughout their adult lives, which enables them to drink animal milk and digest the lactose in it.

Why have some humans retained the ability to digest lactose? Lactase persistence is of course a genetic trait, and it's probably an adaptation since it's such a handy ability to have: milk is an excellent food source, rich in protein and fat, and being able to access this food source throughout your life probably has selective advantages. We also know that lactase persistence evolved recently, in the last 10,000 years, as a result of the cultural practice of dairying, keeping animals and drinking their milk. Lactase persistence is common in populations with a long history of dairying, and scarce in areas with no tradition of dairying.

How did lactase persistence evolve? Keeping animals and drinking their milk presumably set up a new selection pressure acting on dairying populations, providing enormous advantages to individuals who were able to digest milk for longer in life. Natural selection kicked in, and the genes of these dairying populations responded to a new selection pressure introduced by the cultural practice of keeping animals and drinking their milk. This biological adaptation probably then fed back into the cultural practice of dairying, allowing more extensive use of dairy products and further strengthening the selection pressure for lactase persistence, in a self-reinforcing spiral of gene–culture co-evolution.

Lactase persistence is probably the most famous example of human genes adapting in response to new selection pressures introduced by human culture, but it's certainly not the only one. Humans are large-scale niche constructors: like many other animals, we alter our environments and the pressures they impose on us, but we do it on a far greater scale than any other species, thanks to our capacity for cumulative culture. Recent estimates using sophisticated techniques to identify the hallmarks of natural selection in human genetic databases suggest that thousands of genes have undergone selection in the last 40,000 years, probably as a result of changes in human lifestyle driven by our capacity for culture. This suggests that the common intuition that the human capacity to insulate ourselves from our environment means that natural selection is effectively over for humans is almost certainly wrong. It also suggests that the classic evolutionary psychology position, that we have stone-age minds in a modern world, probably isn't true. In fact, this research suggests that the rate of human evolution has *increased* in the last 40,000 years, as we adapt to the new environments our cultures have created for us.

Language: the evolutionary psychology perspective

Let's spend a little time applying these ideas to a specific problem, one of the big questions in understanding human evolution and human uniqueness: the evolution of language. Human language is a uniquely powerful and flexible system for communication, which has no parallels in the natural world. Virtually every species can communicate: flowers signal the location of nectar to bees,

bees communicate with other bees to tell them about the location of flower patches, male birds sing songs to advertise their availability and quality to females, and many species have alarm-calling systems, where they use specific calls to warn group members of the presence of predators. But these communication systems, fascinating though they are, are all quite rigid and inflexible, and can only be used for the limited, specific purpose they have evolved for. For instance, various species have alarm-calling systems, which they use to warn members of their group of predators. The most famous example of this is probably the vervet monkey. Vervets have distinct alarm calls for their three main predators: leopards, eagles, and pythons. These different predators require different types of evasive action (if there's a python around you want to stand up tall and look at the ground, which would not be a good response to a circling eagle), and vervets know which alarm call corresponds to which predator, and act appropriately. This provides a simple, elegant solution to the problem of communicating information about predators among groups of vervets. But that's all this system can be used for: a vervet can't use these calls to reminisce with its friends about the time they saw that leopard, or to discuss what they should do next time they see a leopard, or ask where they should hang out tomorrow.

In contrast, human language is incredibly flexible: basically, anything I can think, I can communicate to you using language (as long as we speak the same language of course!). Languages achieve this expressive power through a series of clever structural devices. At the most general level, languages have *rules*: sentences are built according to a shared set of rules, and if you know the rules of a language and the meanings of the words in a sentence then you can work out what someone is saying, even if you've never heard that particular sentence before. Most of the sentences in this book (including this one) are probably completely novel, one-off sentences of English, which have never been written or spoken before and will never be exactly reproduced again, yet you are able to understand them because you know the meaning of the words and the rules for combining words to convey complex meanings.

Within this basic framework, languages provide devices for conveying all kinds of useful information. For instance, you can encode who did what to whom, in order to convey the distinction between events like 'the dog chased the cat' and 'the cat chased the dog'. You can say when an event happened in time, allowing you to convey whether something already happened, or will happen in the future, or is happening right now. You can convey that an event might happen, or will happen, or might not happen, or won't happen, and you can explain why. You can ask questions that require simple yes–no answers, or request more complex information. Different languages might use slightly different structural devices for doing these various jobs, but they all provide a means to do these things, and much more.

How have humans ended up with such a fantastically rich, complex communication system? One possibility is that language, and all these grammatical devices for communicating complex information, is an adaptation. This argument was made forcefully by Steven Pinker and Paul Bloom in a well-known article titled 'Natural Language and Natural Selection' (Pinker and Bloom 1990). They argue that language is a complex biological trait that appears to be designed for communication. The only way to explain such traits is to appeal to natural selection. Humans live in complex social groups. As discussed above, this means we spend a lot of time thinking about social events, like who is cheating on whom. But it also means we rely heavily on communicating knowledge to one another, both immediately relevant information about current social events or survival-relevant situations and the complex set of knowledge, skills, and beliefs that are needed to survive in the world. Language is obviously well-designed for doing all these things, and therefore language must be an adaptation: the complexity and communicative power of language might be a product of an evolved 'language instinct', a mini-computer or series of mini-computers responsible for acquiring, processing, and producing language.

Language: the cultural perspective

Language clearly involves *something* that's uniquely human, since no other species has a communication system like language, and attempts to teach language to non-human animals have met with very limited success. But we also know for a fact that languages are socially learned – as mentioned above, they are part of culture. You can see that this is the case in your everyday experience of social and geographical variation in language. People from different parts of the world have different languages, and people from different areas within a language's borders have different accents, because they grew up around people who sound a particular way and learned their language based on hearing those people talk. And those people, in turn, learnt their language in the same way: your parents were influenced linguistically by their parents and peers, who were in turn influenced by their parents and peers, and so on, in a chain of transmission leading back tens of thousands or maybe even hundreds of thousands of years.

We also know that languages change as a result of this transmission process because we can see it happen in the written record: the English of today is very different from the English spoken in Shakespeare's time, and the English spoken 1,000 years ago would be completely incomprehensible to a modern English speaker because the language has changed so much. Our historical record of languages doesn't stretch back very far: writing only emerged and developed in the last 5,000 years, and as far as we can tell the first languages which were written down looked pretty much like modern languages, in terms of having rules and structure. But languages have been around a lot longer than 5,000 years: they must have been around, being passed from person to person by social learning and changing as a result, for as long as our species has existed (and maybe even longer, if you think that earlier hominids had language too). This gives language at least 100,000 years to develop, change, and evolve through the process of *cumulative culture* described earlier. It could be that much of the complexity and power of language developed over this time. How could this happen?

We know that, in order to survive, languages have to be highly learnable – they have to make it into the minds of language learners. Learners simplify, regularize, and generally tidy up languages as they learn them. Languages therefore evolve over time and develop rules and patterns that learners can identify and exploit, because those rules and patterns make language more learnable. Terry Deacon (1997, p. 110) has a very nice way of summing this up when he says:

> The structure of a language is under intense selection because in its reproduction from generation to generation, it must pass through a narrow bottleneck: children's minds. … Language operations that can be learned quickly and easily by children will tend to get passed on to the next generation more effectively and intact than those that are difficult to learn.

At the same time, we know that people make conscious and unconscious adjustments in the way they use their language in order to convey the kinds of distinctions and messages they want to communicate. You choose the clearest, or funniest, or most inventive, or most colloquial way you can think of to express yourself. People modify their language to convey the kinds of meanings they want to convey, just as they modify their tools and other aspects of culture to improve the way they function – the only difference might be that, with language, these changes are much more subtle, and perhaps less intentional. But spread over hundreds of thousands of years, these changes, combined with the actions of language learners in simplifying and systematizing language as they learn it, could conspire to build complex, expressive but rule-governed languages.

Just like the classic evolutionary psychology perspective on language this is still just a hypothesis, although it has the notable advantage that it draws on processes that we can see operating in the present day and recent history: language learning, language use, and language change. We can test this hypothesis in various ways: while we can't study the very early origins of language directly, we can investigate experimentally how people learn and use language, and we can simulate these same processes in a computer or using real humans in the experimental lab (e.g. Kirby *et al.* 2008). If this theory is right, then maybe some or all of the features of language that make it so wonderfully useful as a system of communication – rules, word order, case marking, tense, modality, and so on – are a product of culture, rather than a biological adaptation.

Conclusions

Our starting premise was that processes of natural selection have shaped the human brain. From there we presented two different accounts of how this might have happened. The first, evolutionary psychology, says that natural selection shaped a collection of mini-computers, each of which is specialized to solve a particular problem faced by our ancestors in the environment of evolutionary adaptation. Our brains today largely consist in a bundle of mini-computers which are best suited to ancestral environments stretching back up to 2.4 million years ago. The second account suggests that the human brain has evolved significantly in the past 10,000 years. This is as a result of our capacity for cumulative culture which has allowed us to change our environments to be better suited to our needs. Our culturally transmitted niche-constructing behaviours, like dairy farming, have also set up new selective pressures which have driven rapid changes in our genetic make-up. Evolutionary psychology presents a relatively passive view of natural selection, where the organism is constantly reacting to the dangers of its environment. The cultural account, on the other hand, presents the organism as actively altering its environment and shaping the selective pressures acting upon it. This is clearly a caricature of the different views, but it helps to capture the core differences between them.

Humans are unique in the animal kingdom in our capacity for high-fidelity social learning, the sheer amount of social learning we do, and the cumulative culture this produces. Language has clearly played a pivotal role in creating these systems, but again we see a divide between evolutionary psychologists and cultural accounts about how best to explain this. Researchers leaning towards evolutionary psychology will try to find a series of language modules: miniature neural computers that allow us to learn and produce language. Researchers leaning towards a cultural view will look instead at how languages themselves change and evolve, to become easier to learn and more expressive to use.

We've only been able to give a short overview of these positions in this chapter. Research into the interaction between evolution and culture remains ongoing, and provides some of the fiercest and most stimulating debates in contemporary science. The mind may not be a blank slate, but there is a long way to go before we properly understand the nature of the knowledge it contains.

Chapter summary

- There is a debate between nativists and empiricists about whether humans can have knowledge independently of experience. Nativists argue that they can, whereas empiricists claim that the human mind begins as a blank slate, which needs to be filled with experiences. Evolutionary psychology can be seen as one possible modern nativist position.
- Natural selection is a process of environmental filtering, where the environment 'filters out' those organisms least equipped to survive in it.
- Evolutionary psychology claims that human minds evolved to solve the problems of the environment they lived in approximately 2.4 million – 10,000 years ago, a period known as the *environment of evolutionary adaptation*. During this period humans faced recurring problems, and the

environment filtered out those humans without the cognitive capacities to solve these problems.

- Evolutionary psychology maintains that the mind largely consists in a collection of mini-computers, each of which is specialized to do a particular task.
- Evolutionary psychology entails that aspects of the human mind may now be maladaptive: they worked well to solve problems faced by humans during the environment of evolutionary adaptation, but in the absence of those problems in the modern world they can generate unhelpful behaviours.
- Humans are avid social learners: many of the skills we have and the things we know come from learning from others. We call the collection of traits transmitted in this way *culture,* and human culture is uniquely rich and complex.
- Many aspects of human behaviour are products of cumulative culture, the process by which artefacts, social institutions, and behaviours gradually accumulate complexity and functionality as they are modified and passed on from generation to generation. Language itself might be a product of cumulative culture.
- Thanks to culture and cumulative culture, humans participate in massive niche construction: we alter our environments, and therefore alter the selection pressures that operate on us, removing some and enhancing or introducing others.
- Because of the human capacity for niche construction, it has been claimed that human evolution has actually *accelerated* in the last 10,000 years, as we adapt to new pressures imposed by our culturally constructed environments.

Study questions

1   Explain in your own words why evolutionary psychologists believe that our modern skulls house stone-age minds.
2   Can you think of an example of a behaviour that humans have now which might have evolved to solve a problem in the Pleistocene era?
3   What does it mean to say that a behaviour is maladaptive? Can you think of your own examples of maladaptive physical features or behaviours?
4   Explain in your own words how the theory of natural selection accounts for how well organisms are suited to their environments.
5   Why do evolutionary psychologists believe that the brain has to be structured as a collection of 'mini-computers'?
6   Why do evolutionary psychologists claim that a mini-computer which evolved to solve one particular cognitive problem, e.g. how to detect free-riders, cannot be used to solve similar problems, e.g. how to detect the violation of a logical rule?
7   We discussed beavers and their dams as an example of niche construction in non-human animals. Can you think of other cases where a non-human

animal alters its own environment? And can you think of some examples of human niche construction?

8 What is cumulative cultural evolution? Explain it with reference to your favourite piece of technology or social institution.

9 Why do people sometimes claim that biological evolution has effectively stopped for humans? What do you think about this claim?

10 Explain in your own words the two possible accounts of how human language evolved, which one you find more plausible, and why.

Note

1 Although there is plenty of debate in philosophy and other fields about whether the 'mind' is identical to the 'brain', this is not an issue we will be addressing here. Consequently we will use 'mind' and 'brain' more or less interchangeably.

Introductory further reading

Cosmides, L. and Tooby, J. (1997) 'Evolutionary psychology: a primer', Center for Evolutionary Psychology, University of California, Santa Barbara [website], www.cep.ucsb.edu/primer.html (Evolutionary psychology, as defended by its original champions.)

Deutscher, G. (2005) *The Unfolding of Language*, New York: Metropolitan Books. (A wonderfully well-written introduction to how languages change, how they simplify and complexify and what this might mean for language origins.)

Gould, S. J. and Lewontin, R. (1979) 'The spandrels of San Marco and the Panglossian paradigm: a critique of the adaptationist programme', *Proceedings of the Royal Society of London B: Biological Sciences* 205: 581–98. (This is one of the most important criticisms of adaptationist thinking in biology, and the arguments can be applied just as well to evolutionary psychology.)

Hurford, J. R. (2014) *The Origins of Language: A Slim Guide*, Oxford: Oxford University Press. (A short introduction to evolutionary linguistics, from one of the handful of researchers responsible for rejuvenating the scientific study of language origins.)

Laland, K. N. and Brown, G. R. (2011) *Sense and Nonsense: Evolutionary Perspectives on Human Behaviour*, 2nd edn, Oxford: Oxford University Press. (An authoritative overview of evolutionary explanations of human behaviour, including evolutionary psychology, cultural evolution, and other approaches.)

Pinker, S. (1995) *The Language Instinct*, London: Penguin. (An entertaining popular-science introduction to linguistics and the nativist position on language.)

Pinker, S. (1999) *How the Mind Works*, London: Penguin. (An account of how the mind works from an evolutionary psychology perspective.)

Advanced further reading

Deacon, T. (1997) *The Symbolic Species*, London: Penguin. (A fascinating and detailed perspective on the co-evolution of language and the human brain.)

Downes, S. and Machery, E. (eds) (2013) *Arguing About Human Nature: Contemporary Debates*, London: Routledge. (This is one of the best collections of papers on how evolutionary theory affects our views of human nature.)

Fitch, W. T. (2010) *The Evolution of Language*, Cambridge: Cambridge University Press. (A comprehensive overview of the modern scientific approach to understanding language origins and evolution, from one of the leading thinkers and researchers in the field.)

Griffiths, P. and Sterelny, K. (1999) *Sex and Death: An Introduction to Philosophy of Biology*, Chicago: Chicago University Press. (A clearly written guide to evolutionary theory and its impact on philosophical issues, covering challenging material.)

Kirby, S., Cornish, H. and Smith, K. (2008) 'Cumulative cultural evolution in the laboratory: an experimental approach to the origins of structure in human language', *Proceedings of the National Academy of Sciences, USA* 105: 10681–6. (An experimental study showing how language evolution can be studied experimentally, in the laboratory with human participants.)

Odling-Smee, F. J., Laland, K. N. and Feldman, M. W. (2003) *Niche Construction: The Neglected Process in Evolution*, Princeton: Princeton University Press. (The definitive text on niche construction.)

Pinker, S. and Bloom, P. (1990) 'Natural language and natural selection', *Behavioral and Brain Sciences* 13: 707–84. (An influential article setting out the argument that the human capacity for language is a product of natural selection.)

Richerson, P. J. and Boyd, R. (2005) *Not by Genes Alone: How Culture Transformed Human Evolution*, Chicago: Chicago University Press. (A non-technical but comprehensive discussion of cultural evolution, gene–culture co-evolution, and their role in explaining human behaviour.)

Internet resources

Downes, S. (2008) 'Evolutionary psychology' (first published 2008), in E. N. Zalta (ed.) *Stanford Encyclopedia of Philosophy* (Fall 2010 edn (archived)) [online encyclopedia], http://plato.stanford.edu/archives/fall2010/entries/evolutionary-psychology/

Odling-Smee, J., Laland, K. N. and Feldman, M. (n.d.) *Niche Construction: The Neglected Process in Evolution*, Laland Lab, University of St Andrews [website], http://lalandlab.st-andrews.ac.uk/niche/ (An excellent website detailing the theory of niche construction and its relationship to other aspects of biology, including evolution.)

Various contributors (n.d.) *A Replicated Typo* [blog], www.replicatedtypo.com (An entertaining blog with lots of content on cultural evolution and language evolution.)

Walter, S. (2009) 'Evolutionary psychology', in J. Fieser and B. Dowden (eds) *The Internet Encyclopedia of Philosophy* [online encyclopedia]. www.iep.utm.edu/evol-psy/

6 From intelligent machines to the human brain

Peggy Seriès and Mark Sprevak

Introduction

This chapter introduces the idea that computation is a key tool that can help us understand how the human brain works. Recent years have seen a revolution in the kinds of tasks computers can perform. Underlying these advances is the burgeoning field of machine learning, a branch of artificial intelligence, which aims at creating machines that can act without being programmed, learning from data and experience. Rather startlingly, it turns out that the same methods that allow us to make intelligent machines also appear to hold the key to explaining how our brains work. In this chapter, we explore this exciting new field and some of the questions that it raises.

Computations in our head

Intelligent machines are growing in number and complexity around us. Machines search the vast space of the internet to find the precise piece of information we want. Machines read our email to sniff out spam, conversations that are important to us, or possible criminal activity. Machines guess our desires when we shop online, often anticipating what we want before we know it ourselves. Machines recognize human speech and, at least in certain circumstances, offer sensible answers back. Machines pilot aircraft, drive cars, plan missions to space, and explore other planets. Machines predict patterns in the stock market and instigate the movement of trillions of dollars worldwide. Machines read our medical scans and histories to detect the early signs of cancer, heart disease, and stroke.

These are no mean tasks. In many cases, a human would struggle to do at least as well as our best machines. All these tasks have one thing in common: they require intelligent behaviour. They need a machine to follow rules, recognize and generalize patterns, and react rapidly and rationally to new information. Intelligent machines are able to do this courtesy of a brilliant idea: **computation**. Computation involves solving a problem by following a recipe, or set of instructions. This recipe is called an **algorithm**. An algorithm tells a machine how to accomplish its task by taking a series of basic steps.

The steps are often simple – for example, adding 1 to a digit, or checking if two digits are the same. In a computation, many simple steps are strung together to achieve complex behaviour.

Alan Turing (1912–54) was one of the originators of our modern notion of computation. Turing was an English mathematician who was obsessed with the idea of creating an intelligent machine. Turing discovered what he believed to be the key to this in one of his mathematical papers, 'On Computable Numbers' (1936/7). In this paper, Turing introduced the idea of a *universal computing machine.* A universal computing machine is a machine that, if given the right instructions, can take on the work of any other computer. The idea that a single machine could replace every other computer sounds, on the face of it, incredible. One might imagine that a universal computing machine would be mind-bogglingly complex if it existed at all. Turing showed a remarkable result: it is relatively easy to build a universal computing machine. He described a machine known as the Universal Turing Machine. The Universal Turing Machine consists of a paper tape and a mechanical head which can read and write marks on the paper tape guided by simple instructions. A Turing machine can reproduce the behaviour, no matter how complex, of any other computing machine. Given the right algorithm – the right instructions – the Universal Turing Machine can solve any task that any other computing machine can solve. Therefore, creating an intelligent machine should just be a matter of hitting on the right algorithm. In the hands of John von Neumann, Max Newman, John Mauchly, Presper Eckert and others, Turing's idea of a universal machine gave birth to the first generation of general-purpose electronic computers. Today, universal computing machines surround us in the form of PCs, smartphones, and tablets.

The Universal Turing machine is one way to create a universal computing machine, but it is not the only way. After Turing's initial insight, a huge number of different universal machines have been discovered; some are exotic, others mundane. Universal machines are classified into different **computational architectures**, which include register machines, connectionist networks, quantum computers, DNA computers, and chemical reaction–diffusion computers. These devices work in different ways; they have different methods for producing their behaviour. But they share the same universal property: each can solve any problem that is solvable by a computing machine. One might compare the choice between them to that between methods of transport for getting you from A to B: walking, bicycle, scooter, car, helicopter. Each has the same overall effect: getting you from A to B, given enough time, patience, and money. But some methods make reaching your destination quicker, cheaper, or more convenient than others. There is no computational architecture that is universally 'best'. Some computational architectures are more suited to solving certain problems – their algorithms enable a machine to solve the problem more quickly, cheaply, and conveniently – than others.

Much of the work in the project of creating intelligent machines has focused on which architecture is most suited to solve the task of producing intelligent behaviour. Producing intelligent behaviour is a hard problem no matter which architecture one chooses, but some architectures make that task easier than others. For many years, attention focused on simple rule-based systems not unlike Turing's original machines. In the 1980s, attention shifted to algorithms that do not involve the manipulation of language-like symbols, but instead manipulate distributed patterns of activity in networks of simple nodes inspired by the brain ('connectionist networks'; see Clark 2014, chs 2 and 4). Nowadays, the algorithms that hold most promise for producing intelligent behaviour are those that involve **probabilistic representations**. These algorithms are characterized by representing not just a range of outcomes, but also the system's *uncertainty* about those outcomes. For example, a computer would not only represent that there is a tiger lurking around the corner, it would also store how probable it thinks this is. The great virtue of probabilistic representations is that they allow a computer to learn easily by following a principle called Bayes' theorem. Bayes' theorem tells a machine how to update its stored knowledge in the light of new data, and how to make intelligent predictions based on its knowledge. As we will see below, this kind of probabilistic reasoning is thought to lie at the heart of many, if not all, cases of intelligent human behaviour.

The story of machine intelligence, including its most recent probabilistic incarnation, is rich and complex (see Russell and Norvig 2010, ch. 1). We are going to put this story to one side to focus on perhaps an even more significant development that has run in parallel. From the earliest days, computation has also suggested a new way of thinking about ourselves. If computation solves the problem of generating intelligent behaviour for machines, then perhaps we humans work in the same way? This idea – that computation not only explains machine intelligence, but also human intelligence – is called the **computational theory of mind**. The central premise of the computational theory of mind is that intelligent human behaviour is generated by, and should be explained in terms of, computations performed by our brains. In recent years, the computational theory of mind has revolutionized thinking in psychology and neuroscience. Non-computational approaches to the mind exist, and computation may not be able to explain every aspect of our mental lives (conscious feelings are a particularly hard case). Nevertheless, there is widespread agreement that computation provides the most promising story about how humans produce intelligent behaviour.

Levels upon levels

Let's try to unpack the idea that computation could help explain intelligent behaviour. Precisely how might computation enable us to do this? In the 1970s, a brilliant young cognitive scientist, David Marr, answered this question. Marr disentangled three ways in which a computational approach could help us understand the brain. Marr asked *which*, *how*, and *why* questions. *Which* computational task does the brain solve? *How* does the brain solve that task? *Why* is this task important for the brain to solve? Marr grouped these questions together in a slightly unusual way. He began by saying that a computational theory should explain how the brain produces intelligent behaviour on one of three different levels.

Marr's first level is the **computational level**. This level describes *which* computational problem the brain solves and *why* it is important. Imagine that one day you discover a mysterious device in granny's attic. The mysterious device has many flashing lights, buttons, and dials, all of unknown purpose. You recall that granny used the device when she was balancing her cheque book. You play around with the device and you notice a pattern among its lights and dials: if you dial two numbers into the machine, its lights flash out a pattern that could be understood as their sum. Balancing a cheque book requires summing numbers. Therefore, you conjecture, the computational problem that granny's device solves is computing the *addition function*. In Marr's terminology, this is a computational level description of granny's device: a specification of *which* function (addition, subtraction, multiplication, etc.) the device computes. Arriving at this description, as we have just seen, is bound up with answering a *why* question about the device: why – for what ends – did granny use the device? Without a guess about a device's intended purpose (e.g. balancing a cheque book), there would be no way of picking out of the vast number of things the device does (its many flashing lights and dials) which are relevant to solving its problem. This is why Marr groups the *which* and *why* questions together.

Marr's second level is the **algorithmic level**. This level concerns *how* a device solves its computational task. An algorithm is a recipe, or set of instructions, which tells the device how to solve its computational task. Many algorithms compute the addition function. Without further investigation, all we know is that granny's device is using one of them. It may be using, for example, a *column-addition* algorithm. This addition algorithm, which many of us learn in school, requires one to work out sums from right to left: first add the units, then the tens, then the hundreds, carrying to the next column when necessary. Alternatively, granny's device may be using a *partial-sums* algorithm. This algorithm requires one to work out the sum from left to right, storing intermediate 'partial sums' along the way: first add the hundreds treating other digits as zero, then add the tens, then the units, then add the three partial sums to get the answer. Different algorithms involve taking different basic steps, or taking those steps in a different order. Some addition algorithms are faster to run than others; some require less memory. All solve the same problem – all calculate the addition function – but some do it quicker, cheaper, or more conveniently given certain resources than others. The algorithm that a device uses is tied to that device's system of *representation*. Column addition only works if a device uses a *positional* system for representing numbers, such as our Arabic decimal numeral system. If granny's device were instead to use Roman numerals to represent numbers, it could not use the column-addition algorithm.

How do we know which algorithm granny's device uses? A first step would be to look at the resources granny's device has: which basic steps can it take, how much memory does it have, how fast can it execute a single step? Once we know the basic ingredients, we can work out which algorithm it uses. Probe granny's device by giving it a large range of addition problems. Measure how fast it solves addition problems and which kinds of errors it is prone to make. Its distinctive performance profile – speed and susceptibility to errors across different problems – will reveal how it combines basic instructions into a particular algorithm.

Marr's third level is the **implementation level**. Suppose we are satisfied that granny's device computes the addition function using the partial-sums algorithm. We still do not know how the nuts and bolts inside granny's device correspond to steps in the algorithm. Imagine we open up granny's device. Inside we might find different things. We might find gears and cogwheels, electronic components, little pens and pieces of paper, or perhaps a complex and confusing jumble of all three. Marr's implementation level description describes how a device's physical hardware maps onto steps in its algorithm. An implementation-level description pinpoints which parts of the machine are *functionally significant*: which physical parts are relevant, and in what way, to running the algorithm. In an electronic PC, components that are functionally significant include electrical wires and silicon chips: these implement steps in the PC's algorithms. In contrast, the colour of the circuit boards, or the noise the cooling fan makes, are not functionally significant.

How do we give an implementation-level description of a device? One strategy would be to watch the device's workings in action. We could observe physical changes inside granny's device when we give it an addition problem and try to infer how those physical changes map onto steps in the algorithm. Or, we might actively intervene on the physical components inside granny's device – for example, by changing its wiring – and see how this affects its performance. If we damage or replace a physical component, how does that affect the device's speed or susceptibility to errors? By using a combination of these two strategies, we can arrive at a description of the role that each physical component plays.

Marr's three levels are not meant to be independent. The computational, algorithmic, and implementation levels inform one another when we use computation to explain a device's behaviour. Nevertheless, Marr's three levels represent three distinct ways that computation can contribute to explaining a device's behaviour. One might offer a computational theory of an unknown device as a computational-level description (which function does the device compute and why?), as an algorithmic description (how does the device compute its function?) or as an implementation description (how does the physical activity in the device map onto its method for computing its function?). When you encounter a computational theory in science, it is worth asking yourself which of Marr's three levels that theory aims to address.

The situation that we faced with granny's mysterious device is not unlike that which cognitive scientists encounter with the human brain. Cognitive scientists want to know which computations the brain performs, which algorithms the brain uses, and which bits of the brain are significant to performing its computation. Computational theories in cognitive science are offered at each of Marr's three levels. The techniques in cognitive science for answering these questions are not dissimilar to those we saw for granny's device. In order to arrive at a computational-level description, cognitive scientists try to understand the ecological purpose of behaviour (what behaviour produced by the brain aims to achieve). In order to arrive at an algorithmic-level description, cognitive scientists try to understand the basic steps that the brain can perform, the speed that it can perform them in, and how basic steps can be combined to produce algorithms that match human reaction times and susceptibility to errors. In order to arrive at an implementation-level description, cognitive scientists watch the brain, using a variety of experimental techniques (fMRI, EEG, single-cell recording), and see how performance is affected when some of the brain's resources are damaged or temporarily disabled (for example, by stroke or by drugs).

The big difference between granny's device and the human brain is that brains are vastly more complex. The human brain is one of the most complex objects in the universe. It contains a hundred billion neurons, and a mind-bogglingly complicated web of close to a quadrillion connections. The brain performs not one, but many, computations simultaneously, each one a great deal more complex than the addition function. Unravelling a computational description of the human brain is a daunting task. Yet it is a project on which significant inroads have already been made.

The brain: a guessing machine?

Recently, a new hypothesis has emerged regarding the type of computations that the brain might perform: the idea is that the brain might be working like a probabilistic machine, using statistical knowledge to guide perception and decision-making. At the origin of this idea is the recognition that we live in a world of uncertainty. Our environment is often ambiguous or noisy, and our sensory receptors are limited. For example, the structure of the world is 3D but our retinas are only 2D, so our brains need to 'reconstruct' the 3D structure from two 2D images coming from the eyes. Often, multiple interpretations are possible. In this context, the best our brain can do is to try to guess at what is present in the world and what best action to take.

Hermann von Helmholtz (1821–94) is often credited with understanding this. Studying the human eye and judging it to be a very imperfect optical instrument, von Helmholtz proposed that visual perception was the result of what he called an 'unconscious inference' carried out by the brain. Through this automatic process, the brain would complete missing information and construct hypotheses about the visual environment, which would then be accepted as our immediate reality.

This idea of the brain as a 'guessing machine' has been formalized in recent years taking ideas from machine learning and statistics. It is proposed that the brain works by constantly forming hypotheses or 'beliefs' about what is present in the world and the actions to take, and by evaluating those hypotheses based on current evidence and prior knowledge. Those hypotheses can be described mathematically as conditional probabilities, denoted $P(\text{hypothesis}|\text{data})$, which means: the probability of the hypothesis given the data, where 'data' represents the signals available to our senses. Statisticians have shown that the best way to compute those probabilities is to use **Bayes' theorem**, named after Thomas Bayes (1701–61):

$$P(hypothesis|data) = \frac{P(data|hypothesis)P(hypothesis)}{P(data)} \qquad (1)$$

Bayes' theorem is of fundamental importance in statistics: it is sometimes considered to be 'to the theory of probability what Pythagoras's theorem is to geometry' (Jeffreys 1973, p. 31). Using Bayes' theorem to update beliefs is called Bayesian inference. For example, suppose you are trying to figure out whether it is going to rain today. The data available might be the dark clouds that you can observe by the window. Bayes' theorem states that we can get the probability $P(\text{hypothesis}|\text{data})$, which we call the *posterior probability*, by multiplying two other probabilities:

- $P(\text{data}|\text{hypothesis})$: our knowledge about the probability of the data given the hypothesis (e.g. 'how probable is it that the clouds look the way they do now, when you actually know it is going to rain?'), which is called the **likelihood**
- $P(\text{hypothesis})$: called the **prior** probability, which represents our knowledge about the hypothesis before we collect any new information – here for example the probability that it is going to rain in a day, independently of the shape of the cloud, a number which would be very different whether you live in Edinburgh or Los Angeles.

The denominator, $P(\text{data})$, is only there to ensure the resulting probability is comprised between 0 and 1, and can often be disregarded in the computations. In the visual system, in a similar way, a hypothesis could be about the presence of a given object ('is there a bear running after me?'), or about the value of a given stimulus ('the speed of this bear is 30 km/h'), while the data is the noisy visual inputs. The critical assumptions about Bayesian inference as a model of how the brain works are:

- The uncertainty of the environment is taken into account and manipulated in the brain by always keeping track of the probabilities of the different possible interpretations;

- The brain has developed (through development and experience) an internal model of the world in the form of prior beliefs and likelihoods that can be consulted to predict and interpret new situations;
- The brain combines new evidence with prior beliefs in a principled way, through the application of Bayes' theorem;
- Because currently developed intelligent machines also work in that way – learning from data to make sense of their noisy or ambiguous inputs and updating beliefs – we can get inspiration from machine learning algorithms to understand how this could be implemented in the brain.

Multisensory integration as evidence for Bayesian inference

A good model is one that makes predictions. Can Bayesian inference as a model of cognition make predictions that can be tested? This has been the aim of a lot of experimental and theoretical work in the last fifteen years. How our brain combines information from the different senses (for example vision and audition, or vision and touch) is often considered strong evidence for Bayesian inference. Suppose for example that you are walking in the forest, and fear that someone, or an animal, is following you. You can dimly see and hear a rustling of the leaves of the trees. How do you figure out where the animal is located? Do you use one sensory modality more than the other, for example only vision, or both? How does this depend on the reliability of the information available to each of the senses? Similarly, when someone is talking and you can hear the sound of their voice and see the movement of their lips, how do you combine the visual and auditory information to make sense of what they are saying?

Bayesian inference predicts that the best way to do this is to combine the information from both modalities, while weighting the information from each modality according to its reliability. For example, if the visual information is much clearer than the auditory information, it should have much more influence on your experience. This can lead to illusions in situations where there is a conflict between the two modalities, and one modality is much more reliable than the other.

In a lot of situations, it seems that the Bayesian predictions are qualitatively correct. This can be seen for example in the phenomenon known as the McGurk effect, which illustrates how the brain combines information from vision and audition (Figure 6.1A). This effect was discovered by accident. McGurk and his research assistant MacDonald were conducting a study on language perception in infants. They asked a technician to dub the sound of a phoneme (e.g. (Ba)) over a video that was showing lip movements for another phoneme (e.g. (Ga)). They discovered that one would then perceive a third phoneme, different from the one spoken or mouthed in the video, e.g. (Da). Even if we know about this effect, we continue perceiving (Da). This shows that our brain automatically and unconsciously integrates visual and auditory information in our perception of speech,

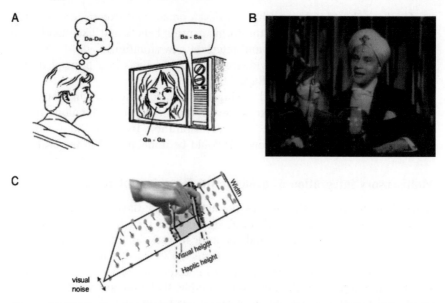

Figure 6.1 The brain naturally combines information coming from different senses. (A)
The McGurk effect. When the sound of the phoneme (Ba) is dubbed over a
video showing lip movements for the phoneme (Ga), we perceive a third
phoneme, (Da). (Copyright image: R. Guski, *Wahrnehmen: Ein Lehrbuch*
(Stuttgart: Kohlhammer, 1996)) (B) Ventriloquism is an extreme example
where visual information completely overwhelms auditory information:
because the source of the sound is quite uncertain, while visual information
about the puppet's moving lips is clear, we end up perceiving that it is the
puppet which is talking and not the ventriloquist. (The ventriloquist Edgar
Bergen in *Stage Door Canteen*) (C) Experimental paradigm used by Ernst
and Banks (2002) to test the predictions of the Bayesian approach. Participants had to estimate the height of a ridge based on visual and touch
information. (Copyright image: *Nature Publishing Group*)

creating a new 'mixture' that might be very different from the initial sources
of information.

Sometimes, though, when vision is much more reliable than audition, it can
completely dominate our perceptual judgements. This can be seen in the
compelling illusion of ventriloquism (Figure 6.1B). Originally used as a religious
practice in ancient Greece (the ventriloquist was thought to be able to talk
with the dead), ventriloquism is defined as the art of projecting one's voice so
that it seems to come from another source, as from a puppet. This is a case of
'visual capture': because the origin of the sound is uncertain, but the lips of
the puppet can be clearly perceived, one attributes the origin of the sound to
the visual inputs, i.e. the mouth of the puppet.

The previous examples show qualitatively that, in everyday life, the brain
combines signals coming from different senses in a way that depends on their
uncertainty. In the laboratory, researchers can perform much more precise

measurements about the validity of the Bayesian predictions. In a seminal paper published in *Nature* in 2002, Marc Ernst and Martin Banks reported the results of an experiment where human subjects were required to make discrimination judgements about 3D shapes (Figure 6.1C). Subjects had to judge which of two sequentially presented ridges was taller. There were three types of trials. First, the subjects could only touch the ridge. Then, they had only visual information: they could only see the ridge. Finally, subjects had both types of information at the same time: they could both touch and see the ridge simultaneously. A different amount of noise was added to the visual stimuli so as to manipulate the reliability of the visual cue. Ernst and Banks measured the smallest difference in the height of the ridge that subjects could reliability detect (aka the 'discrimination threshold') based first on only visual information, then based only on touch information. From these, they could predict quantitatively the performance of subjects for the condition where both visual and touch cues were present, under the assumption that subjects would integrate information from the two cues in a Bayesian way. They found that measured performance was in fact very similar to the Bayesian prediction and concluded that human observers were 'Bayesian optimal'. Since then, this result has been replicated in many different laboratories, using different modalities (for example vision and audition). It is commonly considered as evidence that the brain combines information from different sources in a way similar to a Bayesian machine.

Visual illusions and Bayesian priors

The Bayesian model not only predicts how simultaneous signals need to be combined, but also how to include prior knowledge. According to Bayes' rule, such knowledge can be represented as a prior probability, which would serve as a summary of all previous experience, and which should be multiplied with the new information, the likelihood (see Equation 1). Recently, a number of researchers have tried to explore this idea: if the brain uses prior beliefs, what are those? And how do they influence perception?

Intuitively, it is when sensory data is limited or ambiguous that we rely on our prior knowledge. For example, if we wake up in the middle of the night and need to walk in total darkness, we automatically use our prior knowledge of the environment, or of similar environments, to guide our path. Mathematically, similarly, Bayes' theorem indicates that prior distributions should have maximum impact in situations of strong uncertainty. Thus, a good way to discover the brain's expectations or assumptions is to study perception or cognition in situations where the current sensory inputs or the 'evidence' is very limited. Studying such situations reveals that our brains make automatic assumptions all the time.

Visual illusions are great examples of this. Consider Figure 6.2A for example: despite this image being 2D, we automatically have an impression of depth. Are those shapes bumps (i.e. convex shapes) or dimples (i.e. concave shapes)? You might not be aware of it, but perceiving one dimple in the middle of

A

C

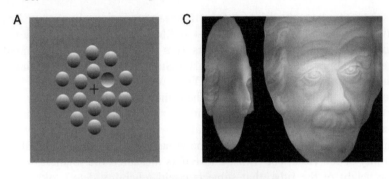

B

Figure 6.2 The brain naturally combines visual information with prior assumptions, leading sometimes to visual illusions. (A) Example of the 'light-from-above' prior. Are those shapes bumps or dimples? Perceiving one dimple in the middle of bumps is consistent with assuming that light comes from the top of the image. Turning the page upside down would lead to the opposite percept (seeing a bump in a middle of dimples). (Copyright image: R. Champion and W. Adams, *Journal of Vision* 7(13) (2007), article 10) (B) *The Ames room illusion*. Here, the brain assumes that the room is box-shaped and thus infers that the height of the people is vastly different. In reality, the room is trapezoidal and the ceiling is not horizontal. (Copyright image: Tom Pringle). (C) *The hollow mask illusion*. The interior of a mask is perceived as a normal face, with the nose sticking out instead of sticking in. (Image taken by Peggy Seriès. Copyright object: Camera Obscura, Edinburgh)

bumps is consistent with assuming that light comes from the top of the image. Turning the page upside down would lead to the opposite percept (seeing a bump in a middle of dimples). The prior assumption that light comes 'from above' has been extensively studied. It is known to play a crucial role in how we view shapes that project a shadow. The fact that the brain uses this assumption makes sense of course, since light usually comes from the 'sun, above us.

Similarly, we seem to expect objects to be symmetrical, to change smoothly in space and time, orientations to be more frequently horizontal or vertical and angles to look like perpendicular corners (Figure 6.2B). We also expect objects to bulge outward more than inward (i.e. to be convex shapes, like balloons or pears), that background images are coloured in a uniform way, that objects move slowly or not at all, that the gaze of other people is directed towards us, and that faces correspond to convex surfaces. The latter is illustrated by the classic illusion known as the 'hollow-mask illusion' where a concave mask of a face (i.e. the interior of a mask) appears as a normal convex face, with the nose sticking outward instead of inward (Figure 6.2C). Here, the bias towards perceiving faces as bulging outward is so strong that it counters depth cues, such as shading and shadows, as well as 3D cues that the brain receives by comparing the information available from both eyes, which signal that the object is hollow. As for the McGurk effect, knowing about the illusion doesn't help: the interpretation chosen by the brain is automatic and unconscious and can't be modulated voluntarily.

Why would the brain use such assumptions to interpret the visual inputs? These prior assumptions make sense because most objects in the world conform to those expectations: light usually comes from 'above' (the sun), noses are always sticking outward, most objects are static or move only slowly, etc. On average, using such prior assumptions thus leads to the best possible guess about the environment. This is why they can be thought of as being 'optimal'. However, in situations of strong uncertainty and where objects don't conform to the average statistics, such assumptions can lead to illusions: we then perceive reality as being more similar to our expectations than it really is. Objects seem slower, more symmetrical, and smoother in space and time, etc.

The Bayesian approach helps in formalizing these ideas. A seminal example of this is the work of Yair Weiss and colleagues. These researchers were interested in the expectation that objects are static or move slowly (which they called the 'slow speed prior'). They postulated that this prior belief could elegantly explain many motion illusions: for example the fact that a line moving behind a circular window (aka 'aperture') is always perceived as moving perpendicular to its orientation ('the aperture problem') or that the perceived direction of motion of a diamond-shaped object (aka 'rhombus') depends on how bright it is compared with the background (i.e. its contrast level). Using a simple Bayesian model where visual information is combined with a prior expectation for slow motion, Yair Weiss and colleagues have shown that they could explain a variety of illusions that had only been explained by independent models previously. They thus offered the idea that visual illusions were not due to the limitations of a collection of imperfect hacks that the brain would use, as commonly thought, or to 'the result of sloppy computation by various components in the visual system' or, but 'rather a result of a coherent computational strategy that is optimal under reasonable assumptions.' They finally concluded that, because they correspond to the brain making very sensible assumptions in a situation of uncertainty, visual illusions could be viewed, paradoxically, as 'optimal percepts'.

A lot of important questions remain. Where do those prior beliefs come from? How are they learned? Are they the same for everybody? Do they depend on the experience of individuals? Can we 'unlearn' the fact that light tends to come from above, or that faces are convex? These questions are the focus of current research. Experimental work combined with Bayesian modelling shows that our brain creates prior expectations all the time, unconsciously and automatically incorporating long-term and recent experience to make sense of the world. For example, after a few minutes of exposure to an environment where some visual features are more frequent than others (for example, objects tend to move in a given direction), we will expect these features to occur again. As a result, we will be more likely to perceive them even when they are not there, or to think that other features are more similar to what we expect than they really are. It has also been shown that the brain can update our 'long-term' prior beliefs that light comes from above or that objects move slowly if we are placed in environments where lights come from below or where objects move quickly. This shows that the brain constantly revises its assumptions and updates its internal model of the environment.

Researchers have also found ways to quantitatively measure the priors used by individuals, and in some cases compared such priors with the statistics of the environment. In general, it appears that the assumptions that people use conform *qualitatively* to the statistics of the world, but that *quantitatively* there is a lot of variability between individuals. This has generated some debates around the notion of optimality: the way the human brain works can be considered as 'optimal' in the type of computation it is trying to perform (i.e. an approximation of Bayesian inference, given the noisy signals it receives) but not always 'optimal' in that the beliefs and internal models it uses can be slightly different from how things really are in the world.

Mental disorders as deficits in Bayesian inference

The idea that the brain functions like a probabilistic machine is not restricted to perception, but has been applied to all domains of cognition. For example, the Bayesian approach may have promising application for the field of psychiatry. It is still very early to say whether this approach will be helpful for understanding mental illness, and there are many competing approaches, which are not all mutually exclusive. However, recent research shows that Bayesian models could potentially help in quantifying differences between different groups (e.g. healthy vs ill) and identifying whether such differences come from using different internal models, for example different prior beliefs, or from different learning or decision strategies. Ultimately, this may help drug discovery.

In the study of schizophrenia, for example, recent work reveals that patients with schizophrenia are not as good as healthy subjects at some probabilistic inference tasks. A task that is often used is that of the 'urns', where participants have to guess from which urn comes a bead drawn at random. In the original version of the task, one urn contains 85 per cent red beads and 15 per cent black beads, whereas the other urn contains 15 per cent red beads and 85 per cent black beads. The beads are drawn one after the other from the same urn, and the participants are asked when they have received sufficient information to decide which urn the beads were drawn from.

Schizophrenic patients are more likely to make their decision after a small number of observations (1 or 2 draws) and to report being certain about their decision after only one draw – a tendency to 'jump to conclusions' which could be crucial for the understanding of delusions and paranoia. Modelling work suggests that this behaviour could be explained by the patients' decision process using less information before committing to an answer, or that would be noisier than in controls.

A common idea in psychiatry is also that the internal models used by patients, in particular their prior beliefs, could be different from those of healthy subjects. In the study of schizophrenia, for example, it has been proposed that 'positive symptoms' (hallucination and delusions) could be related to an imbalance between information coming from the senses and prior beliefs or expectations. For example, using the wrong prior expectations could lead to delusions, while having prior expectations that are too strong could lead to hallucinations. In autism, similarly, it has been proposed that the influence of prior expectations might be too weak compared with that of sensory inputs, which could explain that patients feel overwhelmed by a world perceived as being 'too real'.

In the long run, Bayesian modelling could also help diagnosis. Psychiatric disease or personality traits are usually measured using questionnaires or classification such as DSM-V (the *Diagnostic and Statistical Manual of Mental Disorders* used by clinicians and psychiatrists to diagnose psychiatric illnesses). Coupled with behavioural measurements, Bayesian modelling could help identify more quantitatively the internal beliefs people's brains are working with. For example, Aistis Stankevicius and colleagues (2014) have shown that Bayesian models could help measure how optimistic or pessimistic people are, using a simple type of game where participants are asked to choose between different visual targets. One of the targets is certain: the participants are explicitly told with which probability the target could lead to a reward. The other target is uncertain: the participants have to guess its probability of reward, based on limited previous experience. Optimists expect the uncertain target to be associated with rewards more often than pessimists do, and the amplitude of these expectations can be precisely measured based on the choices of the participants. Such measures could be a complement to the usual questionnaires and have interesting applications in the study of depression.

The implementation of probabilities in neural activity

Bayesian models seem to be very useful for describing perception and behaviour at the computational level (the *which* and the *why*, as explained above). How these algorithms are implemented in the brain and relate to neural activity is still an open question and an active area of research. Whether the Bayesian approach can actually make predictions for neurobiology (for example on which parts of the brain would be involved, or how neural activity could represent probabilities) is debated. It is yet unclear whether the

Bayesian approach is only useful at the 'computational' level, to describe the computations performed by the brain overall, or whether it can also be useful at the 'implementation level' to predict how those algorithms might be implemented in the neural tissue.

Chapter summary

- Intelligent machines that are able to learn from data have become more and more common. To be efficient, such machines need to represent uncertainty in the data, be adaptive and robust. Recently, building machines that represent beliefs in the form of probabilities and update such beliefs using Bayes' theorem has been found to be a particularly successful approach.
- In neuroscience, the idea has emerged that the brain might work in the same way. The brain would represent beliefs in the form of probabilities, and would have developed an internal model of the world in the form of prior beliefs and likelihoods that can be consulted to predict and interpret new situations. The brain would then combine new evidence with prior beliefs in a principled way, through the application of Bayes' theorem.
- Experiments provide support for this idea. When combining multiple sources of integration, the brain does take into account the reliability of each source of information. Moreover, it is clear that the brain works by using prior beliefs in situations of strong uncertainty. The existence of these beliefs can explain a variety of visual illusions, such as the 'hollow mask illusion' or the 'Ames room illusion'. Experiments also show that beliefs about the environment are updated constantly and automatically and can be quantitatively measured in individuals.
- It is still very early to tell but this approach might have interesting applications in psychiatry. Mental illness might correspond to deficits in Bayesian inference, or to the learning and use of internal models that would be different from that used by healthy controls.

Study questions

1 What is the computational theory of mind? Can you think of mental processes that computation would be good at explaining? Which mental processes may it struggle to explain?
2 What are probabilistic representations and why might they be useful for generating intelligent behaviour?
3 Describe in your own words Marr's three levels. How might information at each level constrain the description at the other levels?
4 Why does Marr group the question of *which* computation a device performs together with the question of *why* the device performs that computation?
5 In your own words, describe what Bayes' theorem is about.

6 Explain in your own words how the ventriloquist illusion works.

7 Can you think of a situation where your perception was influenced by your expectations or prior beliefs, so that you had the impression of perceiving something that was in reality not there? Could you try to explain what went on in your brain?

8 Describe in your own words why the Bayesian approach might give us new ways to understand mental illness.

Introductory further reading

Clark, A. (2014) *Mindware: An Introduction to Cognitive Science*, 2nd edn, Oxford: Oxford University Press. (A great introduction to the computational approach to the mind.)

Copeland, B. J. (ed.) (2004) *The Essential Turing*, Oxford: Oxford University Press, chs 9–14. (An anthology of many of Turing's original papers with excellent introductions and annotations. Turing's original paper on universal computing machines, 'On Computable Numbers', is in chapter 1. Chapters 9–14 give a wonderful overview of Turing's contribution to machine intelligence.)

Frith, C. (2007) *Making Up the Mind: How the Brain Creates Our Mental World*, Malden, MA: Blackwell. (Highly enjoyable book that introduces many key ideas in current psychology.)

Russell, S. and Norvig, P. (2010) *Artificial Intelligence: A Modern Approach*, 3rd edn, Upper Saddle River: Pearson. (The classic textbook on artificial intelligence. Chapter 1 has a wonderful and accessible summary of the history of the field.)

Stone, J. V. (2013) *Bayes' Rule: A Tutorial Introduction to Bayesian Analysis*, n.p.: Sebtel Press, http://jim-stone.staff.shef.ac.uk/BookBayes2012/bookbayesch01.pdf. (A very accessible introduction to Bayesian inference and its applications.)

Vilares, I. and Kording, K. (2011) 'Bayesian models: the structure of the world, uncertainty, behavior, and the brain', *Annals of the New York Academy of Sciences* 1224: 22–39. (An accessible review of the current research using Bayesian models to study the brain.)

Advanced further reading

Adams, W. J., Graf, E. W. and Ernst, M. O. (2004) 'Experience can change the "light-from-above" prior', *Nature Neuroscience* 7: 1057–8. (A seminal study showing that the prior beliefs used by the brain are constantly updated.)

Ernst, M. O. and Banks, M. S. (2002) 'Humans integrate visual and haptic information in a statistically optimal fashion', *Nature* 415: 429–33. (A seminal study showing that the way the brain integrates vision and touch is compatible with Bayesian inference.)

Haugeland, J. (ed.) (1999) *Mind Design II*, Cambridge, MA: MIT Press. (A nice collection of essays on philosophical debates surrounding a computational approach to the mind.)

Hohwy, J. (2014) *The Predictive Mind*, Oxford: Oxford University Press. (A recent and accessible monograph describing the theory according to which the brain works as a hypothesis-testing machine, one that attempts to minimize the error of its predictions about the sensory inputs it receives from the world.)

Jeffreys, H. (1973) *Scientific Inference*, 3rd edn, Cambridge: Cambridge University Press.
Marr, D. (1982) *Vision*, San Francisco: W. H. Freeman. (Marr's best known work, published posthumously, and a classic in cognitive science. Very readable and engaging. Chapter 1 neatly describes Marr's three levels of computational description.)
Stankevicius, A., Huys, Q., Kalra, A. and Seriès, P. (2014) 'Optimism as a prior on the likelihood of future reward', *PLOS Computational Biology* 10. (A recent study showing how Bayesian models can be used to study personality traits and cognitive biases.)
Weiss, Y., Simoncelli, E. P. and Adelson, E. H. (2002) 'Motion illusions as optimal percepts', *Nature Neuroscience* 5: 598–604. (A very elegant study showing how a variety of motion illusions can be explained by the brain expecting objects to move slowly.)

Internet resources

Davey, M. (2010) *A Turing Machine in Action: The Classic Style* [website], http://aturingmachine.com
Example of an addition algorithm that uses Roman numerals:
Turner, L. E. (2007) *Roman Arithmetic: When in Rome, Do as the Romans Do!*, Southwest Adventist University [online course material], http://turner.faculty.swau.edu/mathematics/materialslibrary/roman/

The McGurk effect:
[BBC] (2010) 'Try the McGurk effect! – Horizon: is seeing believing? – BBC Two', *YouTube*, 10 November, www.youtube.com/watch?v=G-lN8vWm3m0

The aperture problem:
Anonymous (2013) 'The aperture problem', §4 of 'Motion perception', *Wikipedia*, 6 October, http://en.wikipedia.org/wiki/Motion_perception.

The rhombus illusion:
Weiss, Y. (n.d.) *Moving Rhombus Displays*, Rachel and Selim Benin School of Computer Science and Engineering, Hebrew University of Jerusalem, www.cs.huji.ac.il/~yweiss/Rhombus/rhombus.html

The Ames room illusion:
[*Scientific American*] (2012) 'What is the Ames illusion? – Instant Egghead 23', *YouTube*, 11 October, www.youtube.com/watch?v=gJhyu6nlGt8

The hollow mask illusion:
eChalk Scientific (2012) 'The rotating mask illusion', *YouTube*, 20 July, www.youtube.com/watch?v=sKa0eaKsdA0.
A TED talk by Daniel Wolpert (2011), 'The real reason for brains', *TED*, July [video blog], www.ted.com/talks/daniel_wolpert_the_real_reason_for_brains

7   What is consciousness?

David Carmel and Mark Sprevak

The question of consciousness: philosophical perspectives

Human consciousness is one of the greatest mysteries in the universe. From
one point of view this should be surprising, since we know a great deal about
consciousness from our own experience. One could say that our own conscious
experience is the thing in the world that we know best. Descartes wanted to
build the entirety of natural science on the foundation of our understanding
of our conscious thought. Yet despite our intimate relationship with our own
consciousness experience, from another point of view consciousness is a puzzling phenomenon. We have no idea what it is about us, as physical beings,
that makes us conscious, why we have consciousness, or which creatures other
than humans have consciousness. Not only is it hard to answer these questions, it
is hard to know how to even start to find answers.

What do we talk about when we talk about consciousness?

We talk about consciousness in our everyday lives. We say that 'she wasn't
conscious of the passing pedestrian', that 'he was knocked unconscious in the
boxing ring', that our 'conscious experience' of smelling a rose, making love, or
hearing a symphony makes life worth living. Consciousness is what philosophers
call a **folk concept**: a notion that has its home in, and is ingrained into, our
everyday talk and interests. One problem that we encounter when trying to
understand folk concepts is that they tend to be messy; they collect together
diverse things that interest us under a single heading. When we investigate the
world systematically we may start out with folk concepts, but we are often
forced to refine or abandon them in favour of more precise scientific counterparts. Physics was forced to abandon the folk notions of *heaviness* and
speed in favour of the concepts of *mass* and *velocity*, which allowed us to
describe universal laws and build scientific theories. A science of *heaviness* or
fastness would have been impossible because these folk notions collect too
many diverse things under a single heading. A scientific understanding of
consciousness, therefore, should approach our folk notion of consciousness
with care. Although we use the words 'conscious' and 'consciousness' already,

we might be using them to refer to a variety of different things, and we should distinguish between them. So what might we mean by 'consciousness'?

One thing we might mean is **sentience**. When we say a creature is conscious of its surroundings, we mean that it is receptive to those surroundings and it can act in an intelligent way. For example, we might say that the spider under the fridge is conscious of our presence: the spider is sensitive to our presence and has sensibly taken evasive action. On this conception of consciousness, there is no difficulty with a robot or an amoeba being conscious; it simply means that the entity responds in a reasonable way to its environment.

A second, and distinct, meaning of 'consciousness' is **wakefulness**. When we say that someone is conscious, what we mean is that she is alert and awake: she is not asleep or incapacitated. For example, we might may say that we were unconscious in dreamless sleep, or when knocked out by a blow to the head. This conception of consciousness suggests that consciousness is a global state, a kind of switch, which colours the whole mental life of a creature.

A third thing we might mean by 'consciousness' is **higher-order consciousness**. A creature has higher-order consciousness if it is aware of itself as a thinking subject. This requires not just that a creature have thoughts, but also that it be aware of – be capable of reflecting on – those thoughts. For example, a creature may not just think that it is too hot and act appropriately (take off clothes, seek cooler surroundings), it may also think that having its 'I-am-too-hot' thought is surprising given the wintry weather. 'Perhaps', such a creature may think, 'I am sick, and my "hot" thought has occurred because I am feverish?' Such a creature doesn't merely think about and perceive, it also thinks about its thoughts and perceptions. Higher-order consciousness requires *metacognition*: that a creature reflects on, and thinks thoughts about, its thoughts and perceptions.

A fourth thing we might mean by 'consciousness' is what the philosopher Ned Block (1995) terms **access consciousness**. A creature's thought is access conscious if it is ready to interact with a wide variety of the creature's other thoughts. A thought is access conscious if it is 'broadcast widely' in a creature's brain. For humans, thoughts and perceptions that can be verbally reported are usually access conscious. Not all of your perceptions are access conscious. You have many perceptions and other mental states that you cannot verbally report. The existence of non-access-conscious mental states is one of the most surprising and well-confirmed findings of twentieth-century psychology. Access-conscious states are only the tip of the iceberg in our mental life.

A fifth thing we might mean by 'consciousness' is **phenomenal consciousness** or **qualia** (see Nagel 1974). This is harder to pin down, but it is central to our concept of consciousness. To understand what phenomenal consciousness is, imagine taking a god's eye view of your mental life. There are lots of events taking place inside your head at any given moment. You have beliefs (that

Paris is the capital of France) and desires (to eat lunch soon). You plan (to go to the cinema), and your plans result in motor actions (turning the handle on your front door). You perceive (this book), and you make perceptual discriminations between objects in the environment (between the book and the background). But there is something else going on. Your mental activity isn't just information processing 'in the dark'. It is accompanied by *subjective feelings*. Imagine that a piece of dark chocolate is placed on your tongue. Now imagine that instead a breath mint was placed on your tongue. You could, of course, tell the difference between these two stimuli. But there is more going on than mere discrimination. It *feels* a certain way to taste chocolate; it *feels* a certain way to taste mint; and those two feelings are different. These conscious feelings, which accompany many aspects of our mental life, are what is meant by *qualia* or *phenomenal consciousness*. We currently have no more precise definition than this of what 'qualia' means. The best we can do is gesture at examples. As Louis Armstrong said when he was asked to define jazz, 'If you have to ask, you'll never know'.

Controversies and progress

We have met five things we might mean by 'consciousness'. This is not an exhaustive list; you may wish to think for yourself of other ways in which we use the term 'consciousness'. The list is also a work in progress. The science of consciousness is in its infancy, and it is too early to say whether this is the correct way of splitting up our folk concept into **natural kinds** for scientific study. One particular area of controversy concerns phenomenal consciousness. Daniel Dennett (see the list of internet resources) has recently argued that phenomenal consciousness is not a distinct conception from access consciousness. This is a bold claim: on the face of it, being globally broadcast in the brain seems different from having qualitative feelings (one could conceive of a creature having one but not the other). Many researchers think that access consciousness and phenomenal consciousness are distinct, even if it turns out mechanisms that give rise to them are partly shared.

Let's assume that the unpacking of the folk concept of consciousness above is correct for our purposes. For each of the different interpretations of 'consciousness' above, one might ask the three questions about consciousness that we posed at the beginning of this chapter – what makes us conscious, why do we have consciousness, and which creatures other than humans have consciousness?

Some of these questions turn out to be easier to answer than others. For example, we are making good progress with explanations of what it is about us, as physical beings, that makes us awake, as will we see below. However, one set of questions – those pertaining to phenomenal consciousness – have turned out to be incredibly hard to address. These questions centre on what has been called the **hard problem of consciousness**. Let's take a closer look at the hard problem.

The hard problem

The hard problem of consciousness is to explain how it is that creatures like ourselves have phenomenal consciousness (Chalmers 1995). What is it about us, as physical beings, that produces conscious feelings? Consider yourself from two different perspectives. From a subjective point of view, you appear to know, with certainty, that you have conscious feelings. These conscious feelings come in many kinds: pains, aches, tickles, hunger pangs, itches, tingles, and tastes. Philosophers use the shorthand 'what it is like' to refer to the conscious feeling that tends to occur when we do a particular activity. We might talk about 'what it is like to stub one's toe', 'what it is like to eat a raw chilli', 'what it is like to hold a live mouse cupped in one's hands'. In each case, what is meant is the conscious experience that usually occurs when we are doing this activity. The 'what it is like' locution provides us with a way of referring to conscious feelings that we may not already have a name for. Reflecting on our conscious experience using 'what it is like' reveals that we already know a lot about the nature and structure of our conscious experience. What it is like to taste chocolate is *different* from what it is like to taste mint. What it is like to taste clementines is *similar* to what it was like to taste oranges. What it is like to taste lemonade is *more similar* to what it is like to taste limeade than it is to what it is like to taste coffee. Our conscious feelings have a definite structure and they bear relations to one another. Conscious experiences are not randomly distributed in our mental life. There is a lot to be discovered about our conscious experience from a subject's point of view. The study of conscious experience from a subject's point of view is called 'phenomenology'.

Now, imagine viewing yourself from an outsider's perspective. From this standpoint, it seems utterly remarkable that your brain produces conscious feelings at all. If we did not know this from our own experience, we would never have guessed it. Consider your brain as a physical object. Your brain is made up from over a hundred billion neurons wired in a complex web that drive your muscles using electrochemical activity. How does activity in this network produce a conscious experience? We might imagine, at least in rough outline, how activity in this network could store information, discriminate between stimuli, and control your behaviour. We don't have a full story about this, but we can at least imagine how such a story might go. The case of conscious experience is different. We have no idea where to start to explain how activity in the brain produces conscious feelings. We do not even know the rough shape such an explanation may take. We know, from our phenomenology, that we have conscious experiences and that these experiences have a rich structure. But we have no idea how to explain what it is about us, as physical beings, that produces this.

It is helpful to divide the hard problem into two parts. The first part of the hard problem is to explain why physical activity in our brains produces conscious experience *at all*. Why are we not **philosophical zombies** – beings who have the same behaviour and information processing that we do, but for whom this goes on 'in the dark', unaccompanied by conscious experience? Why do we have conscious experience rather than no conscious experience at all? The second part of the hard problem is to explain, having accepted that we have conscious experience, why we have the *particular* conscious experiences that we do. Why does what it is like to taste chocolate feel to us like *this* and what it is like to taste mint feel like *that*, and not, say, the other way around? Why are our conscious feelings distributed the way they are in our mental life? Both parts of the hard problem are stunningly hard. We don't have anything even approaching an answer to either question. Scientific work on consciousness tends to set the hard problem aside in order to concentrate on more tractable questions.

Why is the hard problem so hard? One diagnosis is that there is an **explanatory gap** between the two perspectives described above: our first-person knowledge from phenomenology and our third-person knowledge from the natural sciences. Both appear to be legitimate sources of knowledge about our mental life. The difficulty is that it is hard to see how to link these two sources of knowledge together. Science has an impressive track record in unifying diverse fields of knowledge. A common pattern in science is to unify fields by **reductive explanation**: by explaining the phenomena of one field in terms of those of another. The kinetic theory of gases, for example, allows us to explain a wide range of phenomena concerning temperature and pressure in terms of the physical laws and mechanisms governing the constituent molecules of a gas. However, past successes at reductive explanation in science have exclusively concerned knowledge gained from the third-person point of view. Pressure, temperature, and the physical characteristics of molecules are all studied from a third-person point of view; we do not gain knowledge of them via introspection. The puzzle here is how to explain first-person conscious experience in terms of third-person studies of physical activity in the brain. There is no precedent for doing this. The task has a qualitatively different character from past reductions in science. A number of philosophers, including Frank Jackson, David Chalmers, and Thomas Nagel have argued that the particular challenges posed by this reduction mean that science will never explain conscious experience in terms of brain activity, and so the hard problem will never be solved. Let's look at Frank Jackson's argument for this claim (see Ludlow *et al.* 2004 for replies).

Thought experiment: Mary the colour scientist

Imagine that a brilliant neuroscientist, Mary, is born and grows up inside a black and white room. Mary has never seen colour, but she is fascinated by the human brain processes that detect and process colour. Inside her room, Mary is provided with encyclopedias that describe everything about the workings of the human brain. These books cover not only current knowledge in neuroscience, but all that could possibly be discovered. From her books, Mary learns every neuroscientific fact about colour vision. She understands in exquisite detail how the human brain responds to colours, and how colour information is processed by the brain.

One day Mary is released from the room. When she goes outside she spots a red rose and experiences colour for the first time. Jackson claims that at this moment Mary learns something new about human vision. Mary learns *what it is like to see red*. She already knows how the brain processes colour, but now she learns what it *feels* like to see red: the character of the conscious experience that accompanies seeing red. Jackson puts it to us that this distinctive conscious feeling is not something that Mary could have predicted from her books. No matter how much she learned about human visual processes inside her room, she would not have known what it is like to see red until she had the experience herself. When she leaves the room, Mary learns, via her first-person introspection, a new fact about the human visual system. This fact was not contained within, or deducible from, her neuroscientific knowledge. Now, Jackson says, if Mary could not have predicted in advance what the experience of seeing red would be like, then we will never be able to explain conscious experience in terms of brain activity. Even if we were lucky enough to have a complete neuroscience, we would at best be in Mary's predicamat. We would not be able to show how the physical facts give rise to phenomenal consciousness. No matter how far our neuroscience progresses, we will not be able to explain how brain acitivity gives rise to conscious experience.

At the moment, science is unable to address the fundamental question of how physical activity yields phenomenal consciousness. A great deal of progress, however, has been made in resolving questions about the sorts of brain activity and psychological functions that are *correlated* with phenomenal consciousness. In time, this growing body of knowledge may contribute to an understanding of the issues raised by the hard problem. In the remainder of this chapter we will review recent findings in psychology and neuroscience that, over the last few decades, have advanced our understanding of these profound questions. We will describe the questions that consciousness science currently finds relevant, and go on to discuss how states of consciousness arise from brain activity, and what determines the content of consciousness – our awareness of ourselves and our environment – at any given time.

Scientific perspectives: the questions consciousness scientists ask

So what sorts of questions do scientists ask when they investigate consciousness? And how much progress have researchers made in turning these questions from general musings into enquiries that can be investigated empirically? The most fundamental question is how the activity of a physical system – the brain and central nervous system – can create consciousness and subjective experience (qualia) in the first place. As we saw above, this is one of the formulations of the hard problem, and science is no closer than it has ever been to answering it. The reason is that we have no idea what an answer would look like; it may be staring us in the face, and we simply don't have the tools – the conceptual framework – to recognize it.

Other major questions are considered 'easy problems', but it's important to be clear about what 'easy' means in this context. As psychologist Steven Pinker (2007; see the list of internet resources) aptly put it, these questions are only easy in the same way that curing cancer is easy – it's not that they are easy to solve, but rather that it would be easy to recognize an answer when we found one. The two main 'easy' questions that scientists are currently interested in both come under the heading of **neural correlates of consciousness** (abbreviated as NCC). Both questions are concerned with figuring out what sorts of brain activity correlate with – i.e. happen at the same time as – processes related to consciousness. The first of these asks what neural activity determines an individual's *state* or *level* of consciousness – what patterns of brain activity lead to a person being awake or asleep, in a coma or vegetative state, and so on. Researchers who investigate this question are also interested in what each of these states means – what level of information processing can occur in the brain when a person is in each state, and to what extent patients with disorders of consciousness, such as those in a **vegetative state**, can still have some capacity for subjective experience.

The second question asks what processes shape the *content* of our consciousness – our momentary awareness of ourselves and of the world around us – at any given point in time? A lot of recent consciousness research has focused on **perceptual awareness** – discovering the link between what the world presents to us through our senses and what we become aware of (you can think of what we become aware of as related to the qualia we mentioned above – but science is currently more interested in what happens in the brain when qualia occur, rather than with how the brain can create qualia at all).

States of consciousness

What different states of consciousness are there?

How does brain activity give rise to different **states of consciousness**? Let's start by examining what states exist. It's useful to think about a person's state of consciousness not as single thing that there can be either less or more of, but rather as a combination of two separate factors: wakefulness (*level* of consciousness) and awareness (having conscious *content*; see Figure 7.1).

Our level of wakefulness determines whether we are awake or not. Our awareness is our capacity to think, feel, and perceive ourselves and the environment around us. This awareness is what allows us to interact with

COMPARING STATES

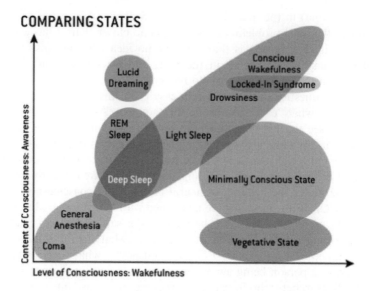

Figure 7.1 States of consciousness. The different states are organized by both wakefulness and awareness. REM, rapid eye movement. (Image taken from S. Laureys, *Scientific American* May 2007. Copyright: Melissa Thomas.)

the external world in a meaningful way. It may seem strange to separate wakefulness and awareness, but as we will see, it enables us to pinpoint the differences between various states of consciousness (Laureys 2007).

Right now your state of consciousness is at the high ends of both the wakefulness and awareness scales; as you fall asleep tonight, you will first become drowsy, and eventually fall into a deep sleep, a state in which both your wakefulness and awareness will be low. Under artificially induced anaesthesia, or trauma-induced coma, wakefulness and awareness are reduced even further. If these were the only states that existed, there would be no need for two separate axes to describe them. There are, however, states in which one of the factors is high while the other is low. The most obvious example is dreaming, where wakefulness is low (a person is asleep) but awareness is high (the person experiences thoughts, feelings, and sensations). In the rare state of **lucid dreaming**, people are not only asleep and dreaming, but become aware of the fact that they are dreaming. Unfortunately, there are also clinical states known collectively as disorders of consciousness, where brain injury leads to reduced awareness during wakefulness. These disorders include the vegetative state and the **minimally conscious state**. Patients in a vegetative state have normal sleep–wake cycles, but when they are awake (with their eyes open) they don't respond to their environment and don't produce any meaningful behaviour (such as following instructions, communicating, or moving in a way that would indicate they know what's going on around them). As far as anyone can tell, they seem to be experiencing no thoughts or feelings. Occasionally, vegetative state patients' conditions improve and they are reclassified as being in a minimally conscious state, a condition in which they occasionally exhibit limited responsiveness to their environment.

Finally, it is worth mentioning the tragic condition known as **locked-in syndrome**. This is not a disorder of consciousness, and locked-in patients are fully awake and aware; their brain injury has rendered them unable to control their body, so they can't move or communicate. Sometimes, such patients retain limited control of a small number of muscles, and can use them to communicate. Some experts estimate that as many as 40 per cent of vegetative state diagnoses may be mistaken, with the patients in fact retaining some awareness but not the ability to communicate (Monti *et al.* 2010).

States of consciousness and the brain

What sorts of brain activity determine a person's state of consciousness? As far as we know, there is no specific brain area whose activity is solely responsible for either wakefulness or awareness. The brain is a vastly integrated system, and its state is the outcome of many subsystems' combined activity. There are, however, brain areas that are known to contribute to specific aspects of consciousness. Wakefulness is highly dependent on activity in subcortical regions (regions that lie deep in the brain, beneath the outside layer, which is called the **cortex**). These subcortical areas include the **reticular formation**, which is located in the midbrain, an area at the bottom of the brain just above the spinal cord. The midbrain is part of the brainstem, an evolutionarily ancient neural structure (meaning it is similar in humans and in many other animals, indicating it evolved long ago in our mutual ancestors). The reticular formation is part of a network of areas known as the reticular activating system, which regulates sleep–wake cycles. Another subcortical region involved in regulating wakefulness is the **thalamus**, which serves as a general relay station for information transmitted in the brain, and is important in regulating arousal (how alert we are during wakefulness). Damage to any part of the reticular activating system or certain parts of the thalamus can lead to coma or disorders of consciousness such as vegetative state, but these disorders can also result from damage to many other brain regions.

Unlike wakefulness, which depends on subcortical structures, the presence of awareness is largely related to cortical function (the cortex is a relatively recent evolutionary development, and is responsible for higher mental functions in humans). Awareness can be thought of as consisting of two complementary elements. The first is awareness of the external environment; this is the awareness we have whenever we need to navigate through our environment, interact with other people, or do anything else that requires the use of perceptual information. Brain regions involved in this type of awareness comprise a network in the frontal and parietal lobes of the cortex, mostly located in the upper-outer parts of the brain's surface. These areas are known collectively as the **task-positive network**, **fronto-parietal network**, or **dorsal attention network**.

The second element of awareness is the kind that occurs when we are not focused on the external environment but on our own inner world – daydreaming, retrieving memories, or planning for the future. Doing these things involves activity in a network of regions known collectively as the **task-negative network** or **default-mode network** (because it becomes active when we're not performing any specific task related to the outside world). This network comprises cortical regions that are mostly located on the medial surface of the brain (the inside part, where the brain's two hemispheres face each other).

When we are awake, we are usually either focusing on something in the external environment or directing our attention inward; it's rare (and some would say, impossible) to be doing both things at the same time. It is not surprising, therefore, that the activity of the task-positive and task-negative systems is negatively correlated – when either is high, the other is low. Although changes in wakefulness are mostly governed by subcortical structures, as we saw above, such changes affect cortical activity, too. As we descend from full wakefulness to sleep, activity throughout the cortex changes. During wakefulness, different parts of the cortex are busy communicating with each other. This is known as functional connectivity, and can be seen in measures of coordinated activity between brain regions. As we fall asleep, this communication is sharply reduced. The greatest reduction occurs in the coordination between frontal and posterior (back) regions of the cortex (note that these are changes in functional, not structural connectivity – in other words, the physical connections between different parts of the cortex remain intact, but those different parts don't communicate with each other as much).

Awareness in disorders of consciousness?

One day in 2005, a young woman was injured in a car accident. She sustained severe brain damage, and was in a coma for a while. She awoke from her coma, but did not regain consciousness. She was diagnosed as being in a vegetative state. Despite having sleep–wake cycles, and spending her days with her eyes open, she didn't respond to any attempt at communication, and made no purposeful movements. As far as anyone could tell, she displayed no awareness whatsoever.

In early 2006, a group of researchers from the UK and Belgium performed a functional MRI scan of this patient. During the scan, they gave her instructions. Some of the time, they asked her to imagine she was playing tennis; at other points, they asked her to imagine walking through the rooms of her house. They had tried this before with other vegetative state patients, but had gotten no response. This time was different, though. The woman's brain activity changed markedly depending on the instructions she got. When asked to imagine playing tennis, her supplementary motor area, a cortical region involved in planning movements, became active. When asked to imagine walking through her house, the activated regions included areas known to be involved in spatial navigation, such as the parahippocampal place area. Most importantly, her neural responses were indistinguishable from those observed in a group of healthy control participants. The researchers concluded that despite the absence of observable signs of awareness, the woman's responses to instructions meant that she possessed a certain level of awareness. They published the study under the provocative title 'Detecting Awareness in the Vegetative State' (Owen *et al.* 2006).

The paper created quite a stir. Was the woman indeed conscious? Could vegetative state patients, in general, be conscious? Critics were unconvinced. The pattern of brain activity seen in this patient, they said, does not necessarily indicate awareness. The observed activity might simply be an indication of how much the brain can do without awareness – perhaps an automatic response to hearing the words 'tennis' and 'house' – rather than evidence that this patient is aware. A related criticism addressed the logic underlying the researchers' conclusions: just because all cucumbers are green, this doesn't mean that anytime you see something green it must be a cucumber; likewise, if imagining walking through one's house leads to a certain pattern of brain activity (in healthy people), this does not mean that anytime you see this pattern of activity it means a person (our patient) is imagining that same thing.

The logic of these criticisms is sound, so the researchers went on to provide a stronger case. In a new study, the same imagery tasks were used – but this time, they were used for communication (Monti *et al.* 2010). Each task was associated with a specific answer. Vegetative state patients were asked simple yes/no questions (to which the researchers knew the answers – for example, 'do you have any sisters?'), and had to think of playing tennis if the answer was 'yes', and of walking through their house if it was 'no'. The researchers found one patient (not the one from the first study) whose neural responses provided the correct responses to questions despite the absence of any beha-vioural evidence of awareness. The researchers concluded that this is reliable evidence of awareness, as the connection between the answer (yes/no) and the actual response (tennis/house imagery) was arbitrary, making it very hard to believe automatic activation could be at play.

This seems sensible, but it is important to remember that the findings do not indicate that all vegetative patients are conscious – out of 54 patients in the follow-up study, only 5 showed differential activity related to the mental imagery tasks, and only 1 was able to use these tasks to communicate. Nonetheless, it seems there is more going on than we previously realized, at least in some cases, under vegetative patients' unresponsive exterior.

Perceptual awareness

So far we've focused on states of consciousness and the brain activity that underlies them. But as we mentioned earlier, consciousness researchers are also interested in the processes that determine the specific content of our consciousness at any given time – our perceptual awareness.

Let's start with our subjective awareness of the environment. Despite normally thinking that we are aware of many different things, research suggests that at any given moment we are only aware of a small subset of the information entering our brain through the senses. There are some great demonstrations that attest to the limitations of our awareness – if you want to experience this yourself, see the internet resources at the end of the chapter for directions to videos made by Daniel Simons and Christopher Chabris (see also their papers from 1999 and 2010). The phenomenon demonstrated in these videos is called **inattentional blindness** (Mack and Rock 1998), and its very existence reveals the intimate connection between awareness and attention. A related, but slightly different phenomenon, known as **change blindness** occurs when no new elements enter or leave the display, but a change in an existing element goes unnoticed.

Hundreds of studies have looked into both inattentional and change blindness, in an effort to figure out what determines the things we are likely to miss. One of the relevant factors seems to be our 'attentional set' – if we're not looking for something, there's a greater chance we won't notice it (for example, have you ever encountered your next-door neighbour in a different part of town, and walked right past them without saying hello just because you hadn't expected to see them there?). Another relevant factor seems to be the capacity limits of our visual working memory (the store of visual information that is available for our immediate use). In studies of change blindness, researchers often present colourful shapes, remove them briefly and return them, and see whether observers are able to notice when one of the shapes has changed. By presenting displays with different numbers of shapes, researchers can find out how much they can increase the number of shapes before people start making mistakes – and the number isn't large at all; it depends on the type of object (and on the specific change), but in most studies it's around four.

Selecting information for awareness

What are the neural processes that choose which information to bring into awareness? When investigating such questions, researchers have made extensive use of a type of stimuli known as **bistable images**. The most well-known example of a bistable image is the Necker cube (see Figure 7.2A), which has two possible visual interpretations, each with a different side seen as being at the front.

The Necker cube has the three hallmarks of bistable images. First, it is a single image that is associated with two possible conscious interpretations; second, these two interpretations cannot be seen at the same time (try it!); and finally, the two interpretations tend to alternate. Another example of a bistable image is the Rubin face–vase (Figure 7.2B). Why are bistable images so useful to consciousness researchers? They provide a great opportunity to isolate awareness from the external, physical stimulus: the image itself doesn't change, but our conscious interpretation of it does. As the only change is happening in

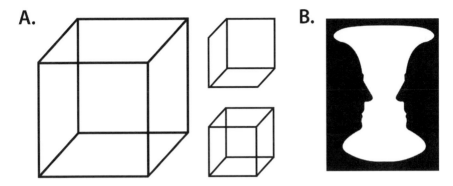

Figure 7.2 Bistable images. (A) Necker cube. (Copyright image: drawn by Carmel)
(B) Rubin face–vase.

our brain, figuring out the neural mechanism for this change would provide insight into how the brain selects perceptual inputs for conscious representation.

Several kinds of bistable images have been used in neuroimaging studies, where researchers examined what changes in the brain are time-locked to observers' reported changes in perception. Repeatedly, researchers have found that during perceptual switches, activation can be seen not only in the visual cortex (which is located in the occipital lobe, at the back of the head), but also in certain parts of the frontal and parietal lobes already mentioned earlier in this chapter (Rees *et al.* 2002). So can we conclude that the fronto-parietal network is responsible for choosing which images enter awareness?

Not so fast. Just because something happens in the brain at the same time as a reported perceptual event (such as a switch in a bistable image), this doesn't mean the brain activity is *causing* the change – it correlates with the change in perception, but correlation is not causation. Let's say we observe activity in parietal cortex at the time of a switch. This could, for example, indicate that rather than triggering the switch, parietal cortex is involved in noticing that a change is happening; or it could be that something else – say, activity in a different region like occipital cortex – caused both the perceptual change *and* the activity in parietal cortex. In order to go beyond correlational evidence, it is necessary to manipulate the factor you suspect might be having a causal effect (in this case activity in certain brain regions), and see how the manipulation affects the thing you're interested in (in this case, perceptual switches in bistable images). In recent years, several researchers have used a technique called **transcranial magnetic stimulation (TMS)** for this purpose. TMS works by applying a powerful magnetic pulse to the surface of the head; for a very short time, this interferes with the activity of the area of cortex directly under the pulse. Interestingly, a series of studies has revealed that applying TMS to adjacent areas within parietal cortex can lead to completely different results – in some cases making the rate of perceptual switches faster, and in others slowing it down (Carmel *et al.* 2010; Kanai *et al.* 2011). This provides strong evidence that parietal cortex is causally involved in bistable switches. But as is almost always the case in research, the emerging picture is more complex than we'd expected: the next step would be to figure out the specific roles of the different parts of cortex whose stimulation leads to different effects, and how the neural system as a whole comes up with a consensus that is represented in awareness.

Suppression from awareness

To understand consciousness, we need to know the differences between processes that require awareness and those that don't. If we can perceive something without awareness, this tells us awareness is not *necessary* for such perception, and narrows down the list of processes awareness *is* necessary for. So how do we investigate unconscious perception? Researchers have developed several techniques that allow them to present stimuli that enter the relevant sense organs, but which the observer does not have conscious access to and is unable to report. One widely used example is **visual masking**, in which a visual image is presented very briefly and followed immediately by another image – the 'mask' – that is presented for longer. People are often unable to report the first image, and may even deny there was one at all. One of the original studies that used masking to demonstrate unconscious perception employed a method called 'masked priming': observers saw words that were followed immediately by a mask (a meaningless pattern), which prevented awareness of the words. After each masked word, observers were shown a string of letters and had to decide if it was a real word or not. Interestingly, people spotted a real word faster when it was semantically related to the masked word (for example, the word 'child' following a masked 'infant'), than when it was not (e.g. 'orange' following 'infant'). This indicated that masked words were processed deeply enough to activate a semantic network in the brain (enabling faster recognition of related words), despite remaining unavailable to awareness; this 'priming' effect was just as large without awareness as with it (Marcel 1983).

A different method, called **continuous flash suppression** (CFS), allows for displays lasting several seconds while ensuring observers do not become aware of what they see. In CFS, a strong – high-contrast and rapidly changing – image is shown to one eye, designated the dominant eye, while the other, suppressed eye views a weaker stimulus (which has lower contrast, but would still be visible if viewed on its own). Under suitable conditions, the weaker image will not enter awareness, despite the suppressed eye being continuously exposed to it (Tsuchiya and Koch 2005). A recent study used CFS to investigate classical fear conditioning with and without awareness (Raio *et al.* 2012). Observers were shown two different pictures, for four seconds each, several times in random order. At the end of the four seconds, one of the pictures – always the same one – was occasionally paired with a mild (but unpleasant) electric shock to the wrist. The participants' skin conductance response (a physiological measure, basically indicating how much you sweat) was measured to examine the development of the characteristic fear response – higher skin conductance whenever the image that predicts a shock is shown. The study included two separate groups: in one, participants were aware of the images; for the other, the images were suppressed from awareness by CFS. Both groups developed a fear response. Interestingly, however, this response developed differently over time: The unaware group's fear response actually arose faster than the aware group's, but the fear learning didn't 'stick' – by the end of the experiment, the greater response to the threatening image had disappeared. For the aware group, learning developed more gradually, but was stable. This qualitative difference – different time courses for conscious and unconscious fear learning – may tell us something fundamental about the role of awareness: we may not need it to form an association between a stimulus and a threat, but for this association to become stable, further processes – ones that involve awareness – may be required.

Theories of consciousness

We still have no idea why neural activity should be accompanied by consciousness at all. However, as we have now seen, science has made quite a bit of progress in characterizing the neural activity and cognitive functions that are associated with conscious experience. This progress has led to a number of theoretical ideas on the kinds of neural processes that lead to subjective awareness. In this section we will briefly describe three of the theories that are currently most prominent.

Global neuronal workspace theory (Dehaene *et al.* 2003) proposes that in order for perceptual inputs to reach awareness, two conditions must be met. First, the activation that the external stimulus causes in 'early' regions of the brain (those devoted to perceptual processing from a particular sense, for example vision) must be strong enough. Second, the perceptual information must be shared with other 'modules' (neural systems devoted to other kinds of processing) across the brain. According to this theory, attention is the crucial process that takes perceptual processing and transmits it to the 'global workspace', where it becomes available to other systems.

A different theory attributes conscious experience to **recurrent processing** (Lamme 2010). This theory focuses on the dynamic flow of perceptual information in the brain. The first stage in perception is a 'feedforward sweep', where the sensory information makes its way up a hierarchy of brain areas devoted to analysing it – for example, visual information is conveyed from the eyes to primary visual cortex, where it undergoes basic analysis; it then goes on to secondary visual cortex for further detailed analysis, and then on to areas that specialize in specific aspects of vision such as motion or colour. This entire feedforward sweep is not accompanied by awareness. However, as it progresses, there is another process that takes place in parallel: feedback loops become active, so that each area that receives input also communicates with the region that sent the information, adjusting and fine-tuning the activity of the previous area to improve the quality of data it sends, resolve ambiguities, or settle contradictions. This feedback is called recurrent processing, and each level at which it occurs contributes to awareness.

The third prominent theory is **information integration theory** (Oizumi *et al.* 2014). Unlike the two theories described so far, which focus on perceptual awareness, this theory attempts to quantify the relation between consciousness in general and the way information is stored in the brain (or in any other system). According to the theory, consciousness is a continuum – there can be more or less of it – and the amount, or level, of consciousness in a given system is determined by how much information it integrates. What does it mean to integrate information? Well, information is integrated when you can't get all of it just by looking at the individual parts of the system. You can have lots of information that is not integrated: a digital camera, for example, can record colour values for millions of pixels, but it is not conscious; according to the theory, this is because there is no integration of all this information – none of those pixels are connected to each other, and no information is passed between them. However, sharing doesn't automatically entail integration: for example, it wouldn't be a good idea for every neuron in the brain to be connected to every other neuron, because then any activity would cause chaos, with all neurons becoming active. The systems that store the most information are those that both integrate information by sharing it, and differentiate this information, making the system's state unique amongst all the possible states it could be in. According to the theory, integrated information and consciousness are *the same thing*. It's important to understand that this is an *assumption* of the theory, not an outcome of its calculations. Does consciousness really come down to nothing more than information organized in a particular way? Perhaps; the theory, however, doesn't lead to this conclusion, but rather uses it as its starting point.

At this point there is no theory that offers a full, unified account of consciousness and how it arises from the activity of physical systems. Current theories offer agendas for future research – what ideas and issues we should be pursuing if we want to understand consciousness. Time will tell whether these directions will turn out to be fruitful, or whether future developments will suggest other directions.

Chapter summary

- The hard problem of consciousness is to explain how our brains produce phenomenal consciousness. We know that we have phenomenal consciousness from our own subjective experience, but we have no idea how brains produce it.
- A number of philosophers, including Frank Jackson, have argued that science will never solve the hard problem of consciousness. Scientific research on consciousness currently lacks the conceptual framework

needed to address the hard problem. It therefore focuses on 'easy' problems (that are only easy in the sense that we would recognize an answer when we found one).

- The 'easy' problems of consciousness that scientists are most interested in concern the neural correlates of consciousness: how does brain activity determine *states* of consciousness, and what neural and psychological processes determine the *content* of consciousness at any given time?
- States of consciousness can be categorized as a combination of two factors: wakefulness and awareness. When we are awake we have a high level of both factors; when we are asleep we are low on both; during dreaming, we have a high level of awareness, but a low level of wakefulness; and vegetative state patients have a high level of wakefulness with a low level of awareness.
- There is evidence from brain imaging that some patients in a vegetative state may retain some awareness of their environment, despite an absence of any behavioural indications.
- Perceptual awareness is the term given to the sensory information we are aware of at any given moment. Despite our subjective sense that we have a rich, detailed awareness, phenomena such as inattentional blindness and change blindness demonstrate that at any given time, our awareness is very limited.
- Bistable images are an important tool in studying awareness, because our perception of them can change without any change in the images themselves.
- A great deal of perception and cognitive processing can occur without awareness. Studying unconscious perception is thus an important way of distinguishing processes that require awareness from those that don't, and of finding out which processes may differ in the *way* they are carried out with and without awareness.
- Several theories have been proposed to explain various aspects of consciousness, though none of them currently offers a full account: the *global neuronal workspace model* and *recurrent processing theory* both offer accounts of the way perceptual awareness arises, whereas *integrated information theory* suggests that consciousness can be measured as the amount of integrated information in a system.

Study questions

1   What is the difference between folk concepts and scientific concepts that pick out natural kinds?
2   What are the various things that folk may mean by 'consciousness'? Can you give a simple example for each?
3   What is the hard problem of consciousness, and why is it hard?
4   What is Jackson's argument that science will never solve the hard problem of consciousness? Do you see any flaws in Jackson's argument?

5 How are different states of consciousness defined, and what determines a person's current state?
6 What is the evidence for awareness in the vegetative state? Is it convincing? Is it possible to know with certainty whether a vegetative patient is aware, and if so, what evidence would such certainty require?
7 What is the relation between perceptual awareness and other mental faculties, such as attention and memory?
8 Why are bistable images useful tools in research on perceptual awareness?
9 What can evidence of unconscious perceptual processing teach us about consciousness?
10 What aspects of consciousness do current theories propose explanations for? And what type of problems – hard or easy – do they address?

Introductory further reading

Chalmers, D. J. (1995) 'Facing up to the problem of consciousness', *Journal of Consciousness Studies* 2: 200–19. (A great description of the hard problem of consciousness.)

Laureys, S. (2007) 'Eyes open, brain shut', *Scientific American*, May, pp. 32–7. (An engaging and accessible review of what is known about states of consciousness and the brain.)

Ludlow, P., Nagasawa, Y. and Stoljar, D. (eds) (2004) *There's Something about Mary*, Cambridge, MA: MIT Press. (This collection includes Frank Jackson's original paper with his Mary argument and many excellent responses. Highlights include the responses to Jackson by David Lewis and Daniel Dennett.)

Mack, A. and Rock, I. (1998) *Inattentional Blindness*, Cambridge, MA: MIT Press. (An influential book that introduced the phenomenon of inattentional blindness.)

Owen, A. M., Coleman, M. R., Boly, M., Davis, M. H., Laureys, S. and Pickard, J. D. (2006) 'Detecting awareness in the vegetative state', *Science* 313: 1402. (This simple, one-page paper reported the vegetative patient whose brain activity indicated she may be aware of her surroundings.)

Rees, G., Kreiman, G. and Koch, C. (2002) 'Neural correlates of consciousness in humans', *Nature Reviews Neuroscience* 3: 261–70. (This review paper is no longer new, but covers the logic and fundamental findings of research on perceptual awareness in an accessible and engaging way.)

Advanced further reading

Block, N. (1995) 'On a confusion about a function of consciousness', *Behavioral and Brain Sciences* 18: 227–47. (Block's original paper in which he draws the access/phenomenal consciousness distinction.)

Carmel, D., Walsh, V., Lavie, N. and Rees, G. (2010) 'Right parietal TMS shortens dominance durations in binocular rivalry', *Current Biology* 20: R799–800. (This study demonstrates that different regions within parietal cortex play different roles in selecting how visual information will be represented in awareness.)

Dehaene, S., Sergent, C. and Changeux, J.-P. (2003) 'A neuronal network model linking subjective reports and objective physiological data during conscious perception',

Proceedings of the National Academy of Sciences 100: 8520–5. (This widely cited paper introduces the global neuronal workspace model.)

Kanai, R., Carmel, D., Bahrami, B. and Rees, G. (2011) 'Structural and functional fractionation of right superior parietal cortex in bistable perception', *Current Biology* 21: R106–107.

Lamme, V. A. F. (2010) 'How neuroscience will change our view on consciousness', *Cognitive Neuroscience* 1: 204–20. (A good introduction to recurrent processing theory, and a detailed description of the challenges facing the cognitive neuroscience of consciousness.)

Marcel, A. J. (1983) 'Conscious and unconscious perception: experiments on visual masking and word recognition', *Cognitive Psychology* 15: 197–237.

Monti, M. M., Vanhaudenhuyse, A., Coleman, M. R., Boly, M., Pickard, J. D. *et al.* (2010) 'Willful modulation of brain activity in disorders of consciousness', *New England Journal of Medicine* 362: 579–89. (In this study, researchers found a vegetative patient who was able to use his brain activity to answer questions.)

Nagel, T (1974) 'What is it like to be a bat?', *Philosophical Review* 83: 435–50. (A wonderfully prescient paper that makes vivid what later came to be known as the hard problem of consciousness.)

Oizumi, M., Albantakis, L. and Tononi, G. (2014) 'From the phenomenology to the mechanisms of consciousness: Integrated Information Theory 3.0', *PLoS Computational Biology* 10: e1003588. (The most up-to-date version of integrated information theory.)

Raio, C. M., Carmel, D., Carrasco, M. and Phelps, E. A. (2012) 'Unconscious fear is quickly acquired but swiftly forgotten', *Current Biology* 22: R477–9. (This study used CFS (continuous flash suppression) to investigate whether a new fear can be acquired without awareness, and showed that it can – but that the learning has a different time course than conscious learning.)

Simons, D. J. (2010) 'Monkeying around with the gorillas in our midst: familiarity with an inattentional-blindness task does not improve the detection of unexpected events', *i-Perception* 1: 3–6.

Simons, D. J. and Chabris, C. F. (1999) 'Gorillas in our midst: sustained inattentional blindness for dynamic events', *Perception* 28: 1059–74. (This study, as well as Simons 2010, use insightful and entertaining demonstrations of inattentional blindness and change blindness.)

Tsuchiya, N. and Koch, C. (2005) 'Continuous flash suppression reduces negative afterimages', *Nat. Neurosci.* 8: 1096–1101.

Internet resources

David Chalmers explaining the hard problem of consciousness:

consciouspictures (2010) 'David Chalmers on the "hard problem" of consciousness – Chronicles of Consciousness', 8 April, *YouTube* [video-streaming site], www.youtube. com/watch?v=kdbs-HUAxC8

Daniel Dennett's recent lecture in which he criticizes the access/phenomenal consciousness distinction:

Dennett, D. (2013) 'Consciousness about access and consciousness', *Consciousness Online*, 15 February [podcast, conference website] http://consciousnessonline.com/ 2013/02/15/on-a-phenomenal-confusion-about-access-and-consciousness/

Great overview of philosophical problems concerning consciousness with many suggestions for further readings:

van Gulick, R. (2014) 'Consciousness', in E. N. Zalta (ed.) *Stanford Encyclopedia of Philosophy* (Spring 2014 edn) [online encyclopedia], http://plato.stanford.edu/entries/consciousness/

The hard problem versus the easy problems of consciousness:

Pinker, S. (2007) 'The brain: the mystery of consciousness', *Time*, 29 January [magazine with online access], http://content.time.com/time/magazine/article/0,9171,15803 94,00.html

Limitations of perceptual awareness:

Simons, D. (2010) 'The monkey business illusion', YouTube, 28 April [video-streaming site], www.youtube.com/watch?v=IGQmdoK_ZfY&list=PLB228A1652CD49370& index=2

Simons, D. and Chabris, C. F. (uploaded by Simons, D. 2010) 'Selective attention test', YouTube, 10 March [video-streaming site], www.youtube.com/watch?v=vJG698U2 Mvo&list=PLB228A1652CD49370

8 Embodied cognition and the sciences of the mind

Andy Clark

What is embodied cognition?

Cognitive science is the interdisciplinary study of the nature and mechanisms of mind. It seeks to explain how thinking, reasoning, and behaviour are possible in material systems. Core disciplines include psychology, neuroscience, philosophy, linguistics, and artificial intelligence. The last twenty years have seen an increasing interest, within cognitive science, in '**embodied cognition**': in issues concerning the physical body, the local environment, and the complex interplay between neural systems and the wider world in which they function.

Work in embodied cognition provides a useful antidote to the increasingly 'neurocentric' (one might even say 'brain-obsessed') vision made popular in contemporary media. We often read about the discovery of some neural region active when navigating space, or falling in love, or riding a bicycle, as if it were itself solely responsible for the ability in question. But what we are really seeing is just one part of a complex web that may include crucial contributions from other brain areas, from bodily form and actions, and from the wider environment in which we learn, live, and act.

In this chapter, we adopt this broader perspective, and examine various ways in which cognitive functions and capacities are grounded in distributed webs of structure spanning brain, body, and world. Such distributions of labour reflect the basic fact that brains like ours were not evolved as 'platform-neutral' control systems: they are not evolved, that is to say, as organs for the control of just any old bodily form. Instead, the brain of a biological organism is geared to controlling that organism's distinctive bodily form and to supporting the distinctive actions that its lifestyle requires. Think of the huge differences in form and lifestyle separating you, a spider, and an octopus! The brain of each of these organisms co-evolved with their distinctive bodily forms, and did so in their own distinctive environments. The best way to get the flavour of these new approaches is by considering some examples, starting with the most basic (arguably non-cognitive) cases and working slowly 'upwards'.

Some examples

The bluefin tuna

Consider first the swimming know-how of the bluefin tuna. The bluefin tuna is a swimming prodigy, but its aquatic capacities – its ability to turn sharply, to move off quickly, and to reach such high speeds – have puzzled biologists. Physically speaking, so it seemed, the fish should be too weak (by about a factor of 7) to achieve these feats. The explanation is not magic, but the canny use of embodied, **environmentally embedded action**. Fluid dynamicists at MIT (Triantafyllou and Triantafyllou 1995) suggest that the fish use bodily action to manipulate and exploit the local environment (water) so as to swim faster, blast off more quickly, and so on. These fish find and exploit naturally occurring currents so as to gain speed, and use tail flaps to create additional vortices and pressure gradients, which are then used for quick take-off and rapid turns. The physical system, whose functioning explains the prodigious swimming capacities, is thus the fish-as-embedded-in, and as actively exploiting, its local environment.

Hopping robots

Next in line is a hopping robot. Raibert and Hodgins (1993) designed and built robots that balance and move by hopping on a single leg – basically, a pneumatic cylinder with a kind of foot. To get the hopper to locomote – to move, balance, and turn – involves solving a control problem that is radically impacted by the mechanical details, such as the elastic rebound when the leg hits the floor. The crucial control parameters include items such as leg spring, rest length, and degree of sideways tilt. To understand how the robot's 'brain' controls the robot's motions involves a shift towards an embodied perspective. The controller must learn to exploit the rich intrinsic dynamics of the system.

Walking robots

Next, consider the thorny problem of two-legged locomotion. Honda's Asimo has been billed, perhaps rightly, as the world's most advanced humanoid robot. Boasting a daunting 26 degrees of freedom (2 on the neck, 6 on each arm, and 6 on each leg) Asimo is able to navigate the real world, reach, grip, walk reasonably smoothly, climb stairs, and recognize faces and voices. The name Asimo stands (a little clumsily perhaps) for 'Advance Step in Innovative Mobility'. And certainly, Asimo (of which there are now several incarnations) is an incredible feat of engineering: still relatively short on brainpower but high on mobility and manoeuvrability.

As a walking robot, however, Asimo was far from energy efficient. For a walking agent, one way to measure energy efficiency is by the so-called 'specific cost of transport', namely the amount of energy required to carry a unit weight a unit distance. The lower the number, the less energy is required to shift a unit of weight a unit of distance. Asimo rumbles in with a specific cost of transport of about 3.2, whereas we humans display a specific metabolic cost of transport of about 0.2. What accounts for this massive difference in energetic expenditure?

Where robots like Asimo walk by means of very precise, and energy-intensive, joint-angle control systems, biological walking agents make maximal use of the mass properties and biomechanical couplings present in the overall musculoskeletal system and walking apparatus itself. Wild walkers thus make canny use of so-called **passive dynamics**, the kinematics and organization inhering in the physical device alone. Pure passive-dynamic walkers are simple devices that boast no power source apart from gravity, and no control system apart from some simple mechanical linkages such as a mechanical knee and the pairing of inner and outer legs to prevent the device from keeling over sideways. Yet despite (or perhaps because of) this simplicity, such devices are capable, if set on a slight slope, of walking smoothly and with a very realistic gait. The ancestors of these devices are not sophisticated robots but children's toys, some dating back to the late nineteenth century: toys that stroll, walk, or waddle down ramps or when pulled by string. Such toys have minimal actuation and no control system. Their walking is a consequence not of complex joint-movement planning and actuating, but of basic morphology (the shape of the body, the distribution of linkages and weights of components, etc.). Behind the passive-dynamic approach thus lies the compelling thought that:

> Locomotion is mostly a natural motion of legged mechanisms, just as swinging is a natural motion of pendulums. Stiff-legged walking toys naturally generate their comical walking motions. This suggests that human-like motions might come naturally to human-like mechanisms.
>
> (Collins *et al.* 2001, p. 608)

Collins *et al.* (2001) built the first such device to mimic human-like walking, by adding curved feet, a compliant heel, and mechanically linked arms to the basic design pioneered by MIT roboticist Ted McGeer some ten years earlier. In action the device exhibits good, steady motion and is described by its creators as 'pleasing to watch' (ibid., p. 613). By contrast, robots that make extensive use of powered operations and joint-angle control tend to suffer from 'a kind of rigor mortis [because] joints encumbered by motors and high-reduction gear trains ... make joint movement inefficient when the actuators are on and nearly impossible when they are off' (ibid., p. 607).

What, then, of powered locomotion? Once the body itself is equipped with the right kind of passive dynamics, powered walking can be brought about in a remarkably elegant and energy-efficient way. In essence, the tasks of actuation and control have now been massively reconfigured so that powered, directed locomotion can come about by systematically pushing, damping, and tweaking a system in which passive-dynamic effects still play a major role. The control design is delicately geared to utilize all the natural dynamics of the passive baseline, and the actuation is consequently efficient and fluid.

More advanced control systems are able to actively learn strategies that make the most of passive-dynamic opportunities. An example is Robotoddler, a walking robot that learns (using so-called 'actor-critic reinforcement learning') a control policy that exploits the passive dynamics of the body. Robotoddler, who features among the pack of passive-dynamics-based robots described in Collins *et al.* (2005), can learn to change speeds, to go forward and backward, and can adapt on the go to different terrains, including bricks, wooden tiles, carpet, and even a variable speed treadmill. And as you'd expect, the use of passive dynamics cuts power consumption to about 1/10th that of a standard robot like Asimo. Passive-dynamics-based robots have achieved a specific cost of transport of around 0.20, an order of magnitude lower than Asimo and quite comparable to the human case. The discrepancy here is thought not to be significantly reducible by further technological advance using Asimo-style control strategies (i.e. ones that do not exploit passive-dynamic effects). An apt comparison, the developers suggest, is with the energy consumption of a helicopter versus an aeroplane or glider. The helicopter, however well designed it may be, will still consume vastly more energy per unit distance travelled.

Passive walkers and their elegant powered counterparts conform to what Pfeifer and Bongard (2007, p. 123) describe as a principle of ecological balance. This principle states:

> first ... that given a certain task environment there has to be a match between the complexities of the agent's sensory, motor, and neural systems ... second ... that there is a certain balance or task-distribution between morphology, materials, control and environment.

One of the big lessons of contemporary robotics is thus that the co-evolution of bodily form, physical mechanics, and control yields a truly golden opportunity to spread the problem-solving load between brain, body and world.

Learning about objects

Embodied agents are also able to act on their worlds in ways that actively generate cognitively and computationally potent time-locked patterns of sensory stimulation. In this vein Fitzpatrick *et al.* (2003) show how active object manipulation (pushing and touching objects in view) can help generate information about object boundaries. The robot learns about the boundaries by poking and shoving. It uses motion detection to see its own hand/arm moving, but when the hand encounters (and pushes) an object there is a sudden spread of motion activity. This cheap signature picks out the object from the rest of the environment. In human infants, grasping, poking, pulling, sucking and shoving create a rich flow of time-locked *multi-modal* sensory stimulation. Such multi-modal input streams have been shown (Lungarella and Sporns 2005) to aid category learning and concept formation. The key to such capabilities is the robot or infant's capacity to maintain coordinated sensorimotor engagement with its environment. Self-generated motor activity, such work suggests, acts as a 'complement to neural information-processing' (Lungarella and Sporns 2005, p. 25) in that:

> The agent's control architecture (e.g. nervous system) attends to and processes streams of sensory stimulation, and ultimately generates sequences of motor actions, which in turn guide the further production and selection of sensory information. [In this way] 'information structuring' by motor activity and 'information processing' by the neural system are continuously linked to each other through sensorimotor loops.

Vision

Or consider vision. There is now a growing body of work devoted to **animate vision**. The key insight here is that the task of vision is not to build rich inner models of a surrounding 3D reality, but rather to use visual information efficiently, and cheaply, in the service of real-world, real-time action.

Such approaches reject what Churchland *et al.* (1994) dub the paradigm of 'pure vision' – the idea (associated with work in classical AI and in the use of vision for planning) that vision is largely a means of creating a world model rich enough to let us 'throw the world away', targeting reason and thought upon the inner model instead. Real-world action, in these 'pure vision' paradigms, functions merely as a means of implementing solutions arrived at by pure cognition. The animate vision paradigm, by contrast, gives action a starring role. Here, computational economy and temporal efficiency is purchased by a variety of bodily action and local environment exploiting tricks and ploys such as the use of cheap, easy-to-detect (possibly idiosyncratic) environmental cues. (Searching for a fast-food joint? Look out for a certain familiar combination of red and yellow signage!)

The key idea in this work, however, is that perception is not a passive phenomenon in which motor activity is only initiated at the end point of a complex process in which the animal creates a detailed representation of the perceived scene. Instead, perception and action engage in a kind of incremental game of tag in which motor assembly begins long before sensory signals reach the top level. Thus, early perceptual processing may yield a kind of proto-analysis of the scene, enabling the creature to select actions (such as head and eye movements) whose role is to provide a slightly upgraded sensory signal. That signal may, in turn, yield a new protoanalysis indicating further visuomotor action and so on. Even whole body motions may be deployed as part of this process of improving perceptual pick-up. Foveating an object can, for example, involve motion of the eyes, head, neck and torso. Churchland *et al.* (1994, p. 44) put it well: 'watching Michael Jordan play basketball or a group of ravens steal a caribou corpse from a wolf tends to underscore the integrated, whole-body character of visuomotor coordination'. This integrated character is consistent with neurophysiological and neuroanatomical data that show the influence of motor signals in visual processing.

Vision, this body of work suggests, is a highly active and intelligent process. It is not the passive creation of a rich inner model, so much as the active retrieval (typically by moving the high-resolution fovea in a saccade) of useful information as it is needed ('just-in-time') from the constantly present real-world scene.

Towards higher cognition

A natural reaction, at this point, would be to suggest that these kinds of reliance upon bodily mechanics and the use of environment-engaging action play a major role in many forms of 'lower' cognition (such as the control and orchestration of walking, hopping, seeing and learning about objects) but that everything changes when we turn to higher matters: to reasoning, planning and reflection. Here, the jury is still out, but a case can be made that higher cognition is not quite as different as it may at first appear.

One very promising move is to suggest that embodied cognitive science might treat offline reason as something like simulated sensing and acting. A nice early example of this kind of strategy can be found in work by Maja Mataric and Lynn Stein, using the TOTO (I'll just treat this as a real name, Toto) robot. Toto used ultrasonic range sensors to detect walls, corridors and so on and was able to use its physical explorations to build an inner map of its environment, which it could then use to revisit previously encountered locations on command. Toto's internal 'map' was, however, rather special in that it encoded geographic information by combining information about the robot's movement with correlated perceptual input. The inner mechanisms thus record navigation landmarks as a combination of robotic motion and sonar readings, so that a corridor might be encoded as a combination of forward motion and a sequence of short, lateral sonar distance readings. The stored 'map' was thus perfectly formatted to act as a direct controller of embodied action: using the map to find a route and generating a plan of actual robot movements turns out to be a single computational task. Toto could thus return, on command, to a previously encountered location. Toto could not, however, be prompted to track or 'think about' any location that it had not previously visited. It was locked in the present, and could not reason about the future, or about what might be.

Metatoto (Stein 1994) built on the original Toto architecture to create a system capable of finding its way, on command, to locations that it had never previously encountered. It did so by using the Toto architecture offline so as to support the exploration, in 'imagination', of a totally virtual 'environment'. When Metatoto was 'imagining', it deployed exactly the same machinery that (in Toto, and in Metatoto online) normally supports physical interactions with the real world. The difference lay solely at the lowest-level interface: where Toto used sonar to act and navigate in a real world, Metatoto used simulated sonar to explore a virtual world (including a virtual robot body). Metatoto included a program that can take, for example, a floor plan or map and use it to stimulate the robot's sensors in the way they would be stimulated were the robot locomoting along a given route on the map. The map can thus induce sequences of 'experiences', which are qualitatively similar to those that would be generated by real sensing and acting. This allowed Metatoto to profit from 'virtual experiences'. As a result, Metatoto could immediately find its way to a target location it had not actually (but merely virtually) visited.

Work on **perceptual symbol systems** (Barsalou 2009) likewise offers an attractive means of combining a dynamical emphasis upon sensorimotor engagement with a story about higher-level cognitive capacities. The idea is that conceptual thought is accomplished using what Barsalou calls **simulators** – in essence, distributed neural resources that encode information about the various sensory features of typical events, items, or scenarios. Thus, the simulator for 'beer', Barsalou suggests, will include a host of coordinated multi-modal information about how different beers look, taste and smell, the typical contexts in which they are found, what effects they have on the consumer, etc. Details of the recent past and the current context recruit and nuance the activity of multiple simulators so as to yield 'situated conceptualizations'.

Simulations and situated conceptualizations enable a system to repurpose the kinds of information that characterize bouts of online sensorimotor engagement, rendering that information suitable for the control of various forms of 'offline reason' (e.g. imagining what will happen if we turn on the car's ignition, enter the neighbour's house from the back door, request the amber ale, and so on). The construction and use of perceptuo-motor based simulators constitutes, Barsalou suggests, a form of 'conceptual processing' that may be quite widespread among animal species. In humans, however, the very same apparatus can be selectively activated using words to select specific sets of sensory memories – as when you tell me that you saw a giant caterpillar in the forest today. Language may thus act as a kind of cognitive technology that enables us to do even more, using the same simulator-based resources.

In thinking about 'higher' cognition and advanced human reason, it may also prove fruitful (see Clark 1997, 2008) to consider the role of physical and symbolic artefacts. Such artefacts range from pen and paper to smartphones and Google glasses, and they now form a large part of the environment in which our neural and bodily systems operate, providing a variety of opportunities for higher cognition to make the most of embodied actions that engage and exploit these robust, reliably available resources. Thus we may argue that just as basic forms of real-world success turn on the interplay between neural, bodily and environmental factors, so advanced cognition turns – in crucial respects – upon the complex interplay between individual reason, artefact and culture.

The simplest illustration of this idea is probably the use of pen and paper to support or 'scaffold' human performance. Most of us, armed with pen and paper, can, for example, solve multiplication problems that would baffle our unaided brains. In so doing we create external symbols (numerical inscriptions) and use external storage and manipulation so as to reduce the complex problem to a sequence of simpler, pattern-completing steps that we already command. On this model, then, it is the combination of our biological computational profile with the fundamentally different properties of a concrete, structured, symbolic, external resource that is a key source of our peculiar brand of cognitive success.

Hutchins (1995) gives a wonderful and detailed account of the way multiple biological brains, tools (such as sextants and alidades) and media (such as maps and charts) combine to make possible the act of ship navigation. In Hutchins' words, such tools and media:

> permit the users to do the tasks that need to be done while doing the kinds of things people are good at: recognizing patterns, modeling simple dynamics of the world, and manipulating objects in the environment.
>
> (Hutchins 1995, p. 155)

In short, the world of artefacts, texts, media (and even cultural practices and institutions), may be for us what the actively created whorls and vortices are for the bluefin tuna. Human brains, raised in this sea of cultural tools will develop strategies for advanced problem-solving that 'factor in' these external resources as profoundly and deeply as the bodily motions of the tuna factor in and maximally exploit the reliable properties of the surrounding water.

Recognizing the complex ways in which human thought and reason exploit the presence of external symbols and problem-solving resources, and unravelling the ways biological brains couple themselves with these very special kinds of ecological objects, is surely one of the most exciting tasks confronting the sciences of embodied cognition.

Simple vs radical embodiment: implications for the sciences of the mind

In addition to asking how far the embodied approach can go, we should also ask to what extent it is a truly radical alternative to more traditional views. To focus this question, it helps to distinguish two different ways to appeal to facts about embodiment and environmental embedding. The first, which I'll call 'simple embodiment', treats such facts as, primarily, constraints upon a theory of inner organization and processing. The second, which I'll call 'radical embodiment' (see Chemero 2009) goes much further and treats such facts as profoundly altering the subject matter and theoretical framework of cognitive science. Examples of simple embodiment abound in the literature. A good deal of work in interactive vision trades heavily in internal representations, computational transformations and abstract data structures. Attention to the roles of body, world and action, in such cases, is basically a methodological tool aimed at getting the internal data structures and operations right.

The source of much recent excitement, however, lies in striking claims involving what I have dubbed 'radical embodiment'. Visions of radical embodiment (see Chemero 2009) all involve one or more of the following claims:

1 That understanding the complex interplay of brain, body and world requires new analytic tools and methods.
2 That traditional notions such as internal representation and computation are inadequate and unnecessary.

And:

3 That the typical decomposition of the cognitive system into a variety of inner neural or functional subsystems is often misleading, and blinds us to the possibility of alternative, and more explanatory, decompositions which cross-cut the traditional brain–body–world divisions.

This is not the time or place to enter into this complex and occasionally baroque discussion (for my own attempts, see Clark 1997, 2014). My own guess, however, is that a great deal of higher cognition, even when augmented and helped along by the use of bodily actions and worldly props, involves the development and use of various forms of internal representation and inner model. These will, however, be forms of inner model and representation delicately keyed to the reliable presence of environmental structures and to the rich possibilities afforded by real-world action.

Conclusions

Embodied, environmentally embedded approaches have a lot to offer to the sciences of the mind. It is increasingly clear that, in a wide spectrum of cases, the individual brain should not be the sole locus of cognitive scientific interest. Cognition is not a phenomenon that can successfully be studied while marginalizing the roles of body, world and action.

But many questions remain unanswered. The embodied approach itself seems to come in two distinct varieties. The first (**simple embodiment**) stresses the role of body, world and action in informing and constraining stories that still focus on inner computation, representation and problem-solving. The second (**radical embodiment**) sees such a profound interplay of brain, body, and world as to fundamentally transform both the subject matter and the theoretical framework of cognitive science itself.

Chapter summary

- Work in embodied cognition explores the various ways in which cognitive functions and capacities are grounded in distributed webs of structure spanning brain, body and world.
- One of the big lessons of contemporary robotics is that the co-evolution of bodily form, physical mechanics and control yields a rich opportunity to spread the problem-solving load between brain, body and world.
- Action upon the world likewise transforms the tasks facing the brain.

- Higher cognition may also depend, in complex and ill-understood ways, upon the reuse of basic sensorimotor capacities offline, and upon interactions between inner resources and bioexternal structures such as pens, papers and smartphones.
- Work in embodied cognition comes in two main varieties: one that sees body and world as merely altering what needs to be computed by the brain, the other (more radical) that sees such facts as transforming our vision of the tools and methods of cognitive science itself.

Study questions

1 In what ways can properties of body, world and action alter the tasks facing the biological brain?
2 Is cognition seamless, displaying a gentle, incremental trajectory linking fully embodied responsiveness to abstract thought and offline reason?
3 Could cognition be a patchwork quilt, with jumps and discontinuities and with very different kinds of processing and representation serving different needs?
4 Insofar as we depend heavily on cultural artefacts (pen, paper, smartphones) to augment and enhance biological cognition, what should we say about their origins? Didn't we have to be extra-smart just to invent all those things in the first place?
5 Is there room here for some kind of 'bootstrapping' effect in which a few cultural innovations enable augmented agents to create more and more such innovations? What might that process involve?
6 What role does language play in all this? Do words merely reflect what we already know and understand, or does the capacity to create and share linguistic items radically alter the way the brain processes information? In other words, to borrow a line from Daniel Dennett, do words do things with us, or do we merely do things with words?
7 Does taking embodiment seriously require us to re-think the tasks and tools of the sciences of mind?

Introductory further reading

Barsalou, L. (2009) 'Simulation, situated conceptualization, and prediction', *Philosophical Transactions of the Royal Society of London: Biological Sciences* 364: 1281–9.
Chemero, T. (2009) *Radical Embodied Cognitive Science*, Cambridge, MA: MIT Press. (A defense of the claim that taking embodiment seriously deeply reconfigures the sciences of the mind.)
Clark, A. (1997) *Being There: Putting Brain, Body and World Together Again*, Cambridge, MA: MIT Press. (Another useful introductory text, reviewing work on embodied cognition from a slightly more philosophical perspective.)
Clark, A. (2014) *Mindware: An Introduction to the Philosophy of Cognitive Science*, 2nd edn, Oxford: Oxford University Press. (General introduction to the field of 'philosophy of cognitive science'.)

Collins, S. H., Ruina, A. L., Tedrake, R. and Wisse, M. (2005) 'Efficient bipedal robots based on passive-dynamic walkers', *Science* 307: 1082–5.

Hutchins, E. (1995) *Cognition in the Wild*, Cambridge, MA: MIT Press. (A wonderful exploration of the many ways human agents, practices, and artefacts come together to solve real-world problems.)

Pfeifer, R. and Bongard, J. (2007) *How the Body Shapes the Way We Think*, Cambridge, MA: MIT Press. (Excellent introductory text written from the standpoint of work in real-world robotics.)

Triantafyllou, M. and Triantafyllou, G. (1995) 'An efficient swimming machine', *Scientific American* 272: 64–71.

Advanced further reading

Churchland, P., Ramachandran, V. and Sejnowski, T. (1994) 'A critique of pure vision', in C. Koch and J. Davis (eds) *Large-Scale Neuronal Theories of the Brain*, Cambridge, MA: MIT Press.

Clark, A. (2008) *Supersizing the Mind: Embodiment, Action, and Cognitive Extension*, Oxford: Oxford University Press. (A defense of the claim that bioexternal resources can form part of the human mind.)

Collins, S. H., Wisse, M. and Ruina, A. (2001) 'A three-dimensional passive-dynamic walking robot with two legs and knees', *International Journal of Robotics Research* 20 (7): 607–15.

Fitzpatrick, P., Metta, G., Natale, L., Rao, S. and Sandini, G. (2003) 'Learning about objects through action: initial steps towards artificial cognition', in Proceedings of the 2003 IEEE International Conference on Robotics and Automation (ICRA), 12–17 May, Taipei, Taiwan.

Lungarella, M. and Sporns, O. (2005) 'Information self-structuring: key principle for learning and development', Proceedings of the 2005 IEEE International Conference on Development and Learning, 19–21 July, Osaka, Japan, 25–30.

Raibert, M. H. and Hodgins, J. K. (1993) 'Legged robots in biological neural networks', in R. D. Beer, R. E. Ritzmann and T. McKenna (eds) *Invertebrate Neuroethology and Robotics*, San Diego: Academic Press, 319–54.

Robbins, P. and Aydede, M. (eds) (2009) *The Cambridge Handbook of Situated Cognition*, Cambridge: Cambridge University Press. (A useful resource including authoritative treatments of a variety of issues concerning embodiment, action, and the role of the environment.)

Stein, L. (1994) 'Imagination and situated cognition', *Journal of Experimental and Theoretical Artificial Intelligence* 6: 393–407.

Internet resources

A general tutorial:
Hoffmann, M., Assaf, D. and Pfeifer, R. (eds) (n.d.) *Tutorial on Embodiment*, European Network for the Advancement of Artificial Cognitive Systems, Interaction and Robotics [website], www.eucognition.org/index.php?page=tutorial-on-embo diment

A video about passive-dynamic walkers:
Amber-Lab (2010) 'McGeer and Passive Dynamic Bipedal Walking', *YouTube*, 18 October [video-streaming site] www.youtube.com/watch?v=WOPED7I5Lac

The current crop of Cornell robots:

Ruina, A. (n.d.) 'Cornell robots', Biorobotics and Locomotion Lab, Cornell University [website], http://ruina.tam.cornell.edu/research/topics/robots/index.php

The MIT Leg Lab site:

MIT Leg Laboratory (n.d.) 'Robots in Progress', MIT Computer Science and Artificial Intelligence Laboratory [website], www.ai.mit.edu/projects/leglab/robots/robots-main.html

More videos of real-world robots in action:

Department of Informatics (n.d.) 'Robots', Artificial Intelligence Lab, Department of Informatics, University of Zurich [website], www.ifi.unizh.ch/ailab/robots.html

Glossary of key terms

absolute space Term used by Newton to indicate an infinite, boundless, Euclidean space as the privileged frame of reference for moving objects (or, what he called absolute motion). Together with absolute time, Newton believed that absolute space was the expression of God's omnipresence (and eternity) in nature.

accelerating universe One in which the second time derivative of the cosmological scale factor, $R(t)$, is positive. A sketch of the expansion would be concave, curving upwards.

access consciousness A thought is access conscious if it is able to interact directly with a wide variety of the creature's other thought; 'widely broadcast' in the creature's brain, and often available for verbal report.

adaptation A feature of an organism is an adaptation if its existence can be explained by appeal to the process of natural selection.

algorithm A step-by-step procedure for solving a problem.

animate vision A frugal and efficient approach to visual processing that depicts the core task of vision not as that of building a rich, action-neutral inner model of a surrounding 3D reality, but rather as the use of active sensing to perform specific tasks.

anthropic principle Any observations we can make are subject to an observer bias determined by the conditions necessary for our evolution and survival. It has several interpretations:

- **weak anthropic principle** Any observations we can make will be restricted by the sorts of physical conditions in which we are likely to have evolved.
- **strong anthropic principle** The universe must be such as to allow life to evolve.
- **participatory anthropic principle** The physical universe's existence depends on observation by consciousness. It may claim support from some interpretations of quantum mechanics, but by no means all.
- **final anthropic principle** Life is essential to the universe's functioning and, once introduced, will endure for all future time and gain all possible knowledge.

antigravity A provocative term for the tendency of dark energy to cause repulsive gravitational effects, leading to accelerating expansion. The term is slightly misleading, in that normal gravity is still assumed – but the quantity in relativistic gravity that causes gravity is an effective density that combines the density and pressure of the matter. Dark energy has a large negative effective pressure (tension), which is necessary in order for its density to be independent of expansion, so the overall gravitational effects are negative.

antinomies of reason Term used by the philosopher Immanuel Kant, and borrowed from jurisprudence, to indicate opposite arguments, presented side-by-side. Kant used the term in his mature work to indicate inconclusive arguments, where opposite inferences are both equally justifiable. The cosmological one, presented in Kant's *Critique of Pure Reason*, concerns the thesis of the world having a beginning in time and being limited in space, and the antithesis of a world infinite in both space and time.

Bayes' theorem A mathematical theorem for calculating conditional probability named after the eighteenth-century British mathematician, Thomas Bayes. The theorem provides a way to revise a prior belief in a hypothesis h given new or additional evidence e. Given new evidence, the theorem says that one's posterior belief in h is the product of the prior belief in h and the likelihood (i.e. probability of getting the evidence e if the hypothesis h was correct), divided by the probability of the evidence, $P(e)$.

Bayesian inference A method of inference in which Bayes' theorem is used to update the probability estimate for a hypothesis as additional evidence is acquired.

Big Bang Solution of Friedmann's equation, which, for expanding universes with sufficiently high matter and/or radiation content, yields a singularity in the past where the density was infinite. Within this model, it is not possible to consider earlier times, and this is the effective origin of the universe.

bistable images A type of image that has two perceptual interpretations, which cannot be seen at the same time and alternate in an observer's awareness. The most well-known example is the Necker cube, an image of a cube that can be seen in two ways, as having either of two sides at the front. Bistable images are useful for investigating perceptual awareness, as unchanging stimulation in the outside world leads to changes in awareness, allowing examination of the processes underlying awareness while the external stimulus remains constant.

causal contact A term denoting that two points lie within each other's light cone, i.e. sufficient time has elapsed that information can be communicated with signals travelling at the speed of light.

change blindness The phenomenon in which an observer fails to notice when an element of a display changes (either between consecutive presentations or during continuous viewing).

closed universe A universe that is of finite volume, but lacking an explicit boundary. This would be the 3D analogue of the surface of a sphere, where travelling in a single direction eventually brings you back to your starting point. A closed universe can also be said to be a 3D space of constant positive spatial curvature. But it is also possible, as first shown by Friedmann, to have negative spatial curvature. This yields an open universe, which is infinite in volume.

computation A problem that is well defined and can be solved by means of an algorithm.

computational architecture A class of computing machines with similar basic steps and ways of stringing basic steps together; members of this class can run similar algorithms.

computational theory of mind The view that (at least some of) our mental life is produced by, and should be explained in terms of, computations performed by the brain.

conjectures and refutations Term used to designate Popper's view of how scientific knowledge develops, starting with (experimentally and theoretically) unwarranted claims, from which empirical consequences are deduced, and tested, which can eventually lead to the refutation of the original claims.

continuous flash suppression A method for rendering visual stimuli unavailable to awareness. Each of the observer's eyes is presented with a different image. One eye (the dominant eye) is shown a high-contrast, rapidly changing image, while the other (suppressed) eye is shown a low-contrast image. Observers often remain unaware of the image shown to the suppressed eye for several seconds, although research shows that in some cases their brain nonetheless processes the suppressed image.

Copernican principle Heuristic 'Principle of Mediocrity', which says that we are not likely to occupy a privileged position in the universe. Named after Nicolaus Copernicus (1473–1543).

cortex The outermost layer of the brain. In humans, the cortex is a recent evolutionary development, and is largely responsible for higher cognitive functions such as thinking, planning and perceptual awareness.

cosmic microwave background Radiation detected in 1965. It originated when the universe cooled sufficiently for neutral atoms to form (at age about 400,000 years). The large expansion factor since then has cooled the radiation to a temperature of 2.725 degrees above absolute zero.

cosmological constant A term introduced by Einstein into his gravitational field equations in 1917. Its effect is equivalent to an energy density of the vacuum, i.e. a form of dark energy in modern terminology. Its effect is to cause an accelerating expansion of the universe.

cosmological principle It says that the universe is roughly homogeneous and isotropic, namely it has the same uniform structure in all spatial positions and directions. More precisely, it says that the observational evidence for the distribution of matter is the same for all observers, no matter where in the universe, and in which particular direction, they might be looking.

crises Kuhn used this term to indicate the transition phase from periods of **normal science** to **scientific revolutions**. A crisis in a well-established **scientific paradigm** occurs when a growing number of anomalies pile up.

culture The label given to a set of **traits** which are acquired by social learning.

cumulative culture The process by which socially learned traits become increasingly complex and functional. Individuals inherit (by **social learning**) a **trait** (a behaviour, a piece of knowledge, a piece of technology) or set of traits, and then modify those behaviours before passing them on (again, by **social learning**) to others. If the modifications that people make tend to improve the function or complexity of a trait, then cumulative culture is the result: the traits become progressively more complex and functional.

dark energy The modern name for the agent that causes the expansion of the universe to accelerate. In practice, very close in its properties to a completely uniform and unchanging non-zero energy density of the vacuum.

dark matter Matter that is detected via gravity only. It is distinct from normal ('baryonic') matter because it does not support sound waves. Possibly some exotic elementary particle.

ecological inheritance Modifications to the environment which persist across several generations.

embodied cognition The study of the mind as a situated system in which considerable work is offloaded to the physical (extra-neural) body and to interactions with the wider environment.

empirical support The support a theory or hypothesis receives from direct *and* indirect experimental evidence. In other words, the overall support a theory or hypothesis receives from all the available evidence when embedded into a larger theoretical framework.

empiricism The label given to the group of views which claim that all our knowledge comes from experience.

environment of evolutionary adaptation The time during which *Homo sapiens* evolved, and, claim the evolutionary psychologists, the era during which the human mind evolved.

environmentally embedded action A purposive behaviour (such as driving a car) undertaken in a distinctive task-relevant setting. For example, driving the car along roads marked with white lines, signage, etc.

event horizon In some circumstances, a given point in space may be unable to send signals at the speed of light to some parts of space, even in the limit of infinite future time. There is then said to be an event horizon at the maximum distance that can be reached. An event horizon exists in a universe with accelerating expansion, where distant regions are genuinely moving away from us faster than light.

evolutionary psychology A research program which maintains that the brains we have now are actually adapted to suit problems which humans faced during the **environment of evolutionary adaptation**.

expanding space A common misconception. On scales smaller than the curvature radius of spacetime, the expansion of the universe cannot be detected. There is no local 'stretching' associated with the expansion of the universe; this would be inconsistent with the fundamentals of general relativity.

explanatory gap Gap between knowledge of phenomenal consciousness from a first-person point of view (gained via introspection) and that from a third-person point of view (gained via study of the brain).

falsification Popper's criterion for demarcating scientific theories from pseudo-scientific theories. Scientific theories should be able to make risky novel predictions that can be falsified with one single piece of negative evidence.

Fermi's paradox The tension between the apparently high likelihood that advanced extraterrestrial life exists (e.g. given the universe's age and diversity of stars) and the lack of evidence that such life exists. Named after physicist Enrico Fermi (1901–54).

folk concept Way of grouping of entities that arises out of our everyday talk; often groups entities together in a way that reflects human interests and values rather than an intrinsic feature they have in common.

global neuronal workspace theory A theory of consciousness, which proposes that for a perceptual experience to reach awareness, it must cause activation not only in the perceptual system devoted to it (e.g. visual cortex being activated in response to a visual stimulus), but be transmitted widely across the brain, becoming available in a 'global workspace' where it is shared with other neural systems.

hard problem of consciousness Problem of explaining how physical activity in the brain gives rise to phenomenal consciousness.

higher-order consciousness Awareness of one's own mental states; ability to reflect on one's thoughts and perceptions.

horizon distance The name for the separation of points that have just been able to come into causal contact at a given time in the universe. In a standard Big Bang model, the horizon distance is finite, but it grows with time. If the universe decelerates, then the horizon distance grows without limit, and all points will eventually come into causal contact. But in an accelerating universe, the horizon distance has a maximum value, which is the event horizon. In this case, sufficiently wide separated points can never exchange light signals.

horizon problem The horizon distance in standard Big Bang cosmology is small, but increases with time. There is therefore a difficulty in understanding how the universe can be so uniform on large scales, even though there has apparently been insufficient time for causal processes to agree in matters such as the mean density of the universe. Inflationary cosmology is the most popular means of solving this problem.

Hubble constant The constant of proportionality between distance and redshift. Its modern value is close to $70 \text{ km s}^{-1} \text{ Mpc}^{-1}$.

inattentional blindness The phenomenon in which an observer fails to notice a new element that enters a display (or an old element that leaves it) when the observer's attention is engaged with other elements of the display.

incommensurability Two scientific theories are incommensurable when there is no basis common to both theories, on which they may be assessed (because the two theories lack common conceptual, methodological and experimental resources, among others).

inductivism The view that identifies the scientific method with the inductive method. On this view, scientific knowledge would proceed from many positive instances (with no negative instances) to a universal generalization about the phenomenon under investigation.

inflation The idea that the early universe expanded exponentially, driven by the energy density of a scalar field like the Higgs field, known as the inflaton.

inflationary cosmology An attempt from the early 1980s to explain the origin of the expanding universe without the Big Bang singularity. It relies on the idea that the dark energy density could have been much larger at early times, accelerating the universe into motion.

information integration theory A theory of consciousness, which proposes that consciousness is a function of information integration within a system.

Information is considered 'integrated' when it is shared by different parts of the system, and cannot be completely described by just collecting the information contained in the system's individual elements.

innate Broadly speaking, some cognitive capacity is innate if it is not learned.

Kant–Laplace nebular hypothesis This is the hypothesis, first formulated by Kant in 1755, and later developed by Laplace, about the planets and stars forming from an original nebula of gases. In Kant's original formulation, space at the origin was filled with a 'fine matter' on which two fundamental forces of attraction and repulsion acted to form nucleation sites for planets and stars.

lactase persistence Retaining the ability to digest lactose (the sugar in milk) past the point of weaning. This is a rare trait in mammals, but is observed in a minority of the world's population, as an evolutionary response to the cultural practice of dairying.

landscape The idea, derived from string theory, that there are many scalar fields, and many potential minima, up to 10^{500} of them, allowing the possibility that rare minima can lie at the level of the observed vacuum density.

last scattering surface The point of origin of the CMB (cosmic microwave background) radiation. Plasma at a temperature around 3,000 degrees, just at the stage of becoming neutral.

ΛCDM model Called also the concordance model. The standard cosmological framework, in which the universe is dominated by (collisionless and cold) dark matter and dark energy, with the latter behaving in the same way as Einstein's **cosmological constant**, Λ.

Leibniz's principle of plenitude Metaphysical principle introduced by the German philosopher G. W. Leibniz to indicate that everything that can possibly exist, will indeed exist. The principle implies that nature forms a continuum in its hierarchy of beings, with no gaps or jumps.

Likelihood function, or **likelihood** In statistics, it is the probability of the observed evidence e given the hypothesis h, namely $P(e|h)$. It is commonly described as the 'evidence' for the hypothesis.

locked-in syndrome A condition in which, as a result of brain trauma (often a stroke), a person remains completely conscious but loses the ability to control all (or nearly all) muscles, leading to an inability to communicate. Some locked-in patients retain control of a small number of muscles (e.g. an eyelid) and can use those to communicate.

lucid dreaming The condition of being aware that one is currently dreaming.

maladaptation A maladaptive trait evolved due to certain evolutionary pressures that have since changed, causing the trait to be detrimental rather than beneficial to the organism.

Marr's algorithmic level Description of how a device computes its function.

Marr's computational level Description of which function a device computes and why the device computes that function.

Marr's implementation level Description of which physical properties of the device are relevant to it computing its function and the role that each of those physical properties plays.

methodological anarchism This is the name that the philosopher Paul Feyerabend gave to his own position, as a radical view that denies any distinctive methodology, or algorithm, or set of rules for science.

minimally conscious state A disorder of consciousness, in which patients (often the survivors of a stroke or head trauma) are largely unresponsive but exhibit occasional indications that they are aware of themselves and their surroundings, such as following motion with their eyes or responding to instructions to make simple movements. Patients often progress to a minimally conscious state from previously being in a vegetative state.

modified gravity The idea that general relativity gives a correct description of relativistic gravity only on scales of the solar system, but that a different theory applies on cosmological scales. Thus dark energy might not be a physical substance, but an artefact of assuming the incorrect theory of gravity.

modularity theory The theory that the human brain is largely structured as a collection of specialized mini-computers.

multiverse An ensemble, postulated by several physical and philosophical theories, of many distinct, concrete universes. The multiverse would comprise all physical reality and (in many versions) contain every physically possible arrangement of space, time, matter and energy. (In some versions, the multiverse contains all mathematically or logically possible universes too.)

nativism The label given to the group of views, which maintain that we can have some knowledge independently of experience.

natural kind A grouping of entities that does not depend on humans or their interests, but reflects the way that those entities are grouped by nature into categories governed by laws or natural processes.

natural selection The theory that organized biological complexity can be explained by non-intentional but non-random selection (according to adaptive fitness) of traits generated through random mutation. First developed by Charles Darwin (1809–82) in *The Origin of Species* (1859). A feature of an organism is a product of natural selection if (a) it is heritable; (b) there is historical variation in a species regarding that feature (some had it and some did not); (c) having the feature confers a survival or reproductive advantage on the organism which has it.

neural correlates of consciousness The minimal set of events in the nervous system that is sufficient for a conscious experience to arise.

niche construction The process by which organisms, through their own behaviour, modify their own environment or the environment of others.

normal science The philosopher Thomas Kuhn referred with this term to periods of scientific activity (spanning often centuries) where the scientific community works within a well-defined **scientific paradigm**, and most of the activity consists in puzzle-solving (e.g. finding solutions to well-defined problems within an accepted paradigm).

Ockham's razor Principle of *ontological parsimony*: 'Entities are not to be multiplied beyond necessity'. It urges simplicity in choosing explanations – use only the minimal number of entities (or principles) which suffice. Named after William of Ockham (*c.* 1285–1347).

passive dynamics The dynamical behaviour of a system when disconnected from energy supplies such as batteries, mains power, steam power, etc.

past light cone The set of points in space from which signals sent at the speed of light are just reaching us now. The observed universe lies 'within' the light cone.

perceptual awareness The content of consciousness that is a representation of the external world; the subset of sensations entering perceptual systems (such as the visual or auditory systems) that are available to consciousness at a specific moment.

perceptual symbol systems approach An approach to higher cognition that relies upon the use of sensory simulations, so that we reason about the world using many of the same resources that are engaged by online perception and action.

phenomenal consciousness Subjective feelings that accompany many aspects of human mental life. Examples include pains, aches, tickles, hunger pangs, itches, tingles and tastes.

philosophical zombie Hypothetical entity with the same behaviour, information processing and physical make-up as ourselves but lacking phenomenal consciousness.

potential falsifiers Popper used this term to designate risky novel predictions, which if proved wrong, have the power to falsify the conjecture at stake. The higher the number of potential falsifiers, the higher the scientific status of the conjecture.

primordial nucleosynthesis The theory in which the light chemical elements (especially deuterium and helium) were synthesized by nuclear reactions at temperatures around 10^{10} degrees, and times in the order of seconds to minutes. This theory can account for why all stars have about 25 per cent of their mass in the form of helium.

principle of general relativity Also known as the principle of general covariance. The idea that valid laws of physics must take a form that is independent of coordinates and so valid for all observers, independently of their state of motion.

prior probability distribution, or **prior**, of an uncertain hypothesis h is the probability distribution $P(h)$ that expresses one's personal degree of belief about h before any new evidence is collected.

probabilistic representation A representation that includes a measure of uncertainty about it being true.

qualia See **phenomenal consciousness**

radical embodiment The idea that taking facts about the role of body and world seriously requires us to reconceive both the subject matter and the methods and constructs of cognitive science.

recurrent processing theory A theory of consciousness which proposes that perception propagates through the brain in an initial 'feedforward sweep', from early perceptual to 'higher' cognitive areas; this propagation occurs without awareness, but is accompanied by feedback from higher areas to lower ones, and it is this 'recurrent' processing that is required for a conscious perceptual experience to arise.

redshift The displacement of spectral features to long wavelength from the expansion of the universe. Usually denoted z, the stretch factor in wavelength is $1 + z$. For small redshifts, the correct interpretation is as a Doppler shift in terms of a recessional velocity v, where $z = v/c$ and c is the speed of light.

reductionism The philosophical view that claims that whenever there are many levels in the explanation of a given phenomenon, it is possible to reduce higher levels to lower (presumably more fundamental and irreducible) ones. The term applies to different contexts of discourse and explanation (a classic example being the reduction of biological phenomena to physical phenomena).

reductive explanation Explaining phenomena in one scientific domain by the activities of entities in another domain; a reductive explanation should demonstrate how the former phenomena are entirely determined by the activities of the entities of the latter domain.

relics This is a generic term for objects that exist in the present-day universe as a residue of a population that was much more abundant at early times. The most common example is the annihilation of massive particles and antiparticles, which can leave a small number that have failed to annihilate.

reticular formation A region in the brain stem that is involved in regulating states of consciousness and sleep–wake cycles.

scalar field Quantum mechanical field whose corresponding particle has spin zero. It means there is some constituent of nature that is characterized purely by a single number (a scalar) at any given point in space. Variations in the value or rate of change of a scalar field can cause a change in energy density. The only known fundamental scalar field is the Higgs field from particle physics. But inflationary cosmology assumes there is another such field, the inflaton: slow changes in the inflaton can mimic dark energy.

scale factor In a uniformly expanding universe, all separations between galaxies increase by the same factor in a given time. Thus they are proportional to a universal function of time, $R(t)$. The value of this function is a length, denoting the radius over which spacetime curvature is perceptible. The logarithmic time derivative, $(dR/dt)/R$, yields H – the constant of proportionality in Hubble's law.

scientific paradigm Term used by Thomas Kuhn to indicate the theoretical and experimental resources, methodology and system of values endorsed by a scientific community at any given time in the history of science.

scientific realism Scientific realism is the view that says that science aims to give us a literally true story about nature. A scientific realist typically endorses the following three claims: (a) that nature (and its objects and entities) exist mind-independently (metaphysical aspect); (b) that our best scientific theories are true, i.e. what they say about nature and its objects corresponds to the way nature is (epistemic aspect); (c) that scientific language refers to or picks out objects existing mind-independently in nature (semantic aspect). Typically a realist sees science as progressing towards better and better theories, which are closer to the truth (or approximately true).

scientific revolutions Term used by Kuhn to indicate periods in the history of science where a sufficient number of anomalies accumulate to challenge the accepted scientific paradigm, and a rival paradigm comes to the fore, around which scientific consensus gathers.

sentience Being receptive to surroundings and responding to them in an intelligent way.

simple embodiment The idea that facts about body and world constrain the inner organizations that are the subject matter of cognitive science.

simulator As used by Larry Barsalou, a simulator is a set of neural resources that together encode information about the various sensory features of typical events, items, or scenarios. Such linked resources may then be used to recreate (simulate) those characteristic neural activity patterns even in the absence of the item or state of affairs.

social learning Learning from the behaviour of others. This could be through teaching, through imitation, or through more subtle social influences on behaviour.

standard candles, or **standard rulers** Astronomical objects that can be treated as identical in energy output or in size at all times. Then the inverse-square law can be used to infer relative distances from relative apparent brightness. Type Ia supernovae are the best-known examples.

states of consciousness A conscious being's current state is determined by a combination of two factors – wakefulness (whether they are awake or not) and awareness (whether they have any conscious content concerning themselves or the external world).

steady-state universe A model promoted by Bondi, Gold and Hoyle in the 1960s, in which the expansion appeared the same at all times, so there was no Big Bang. Disproved most directly by detection of the CMB (cosmic microwave background).

string theory A speculative theory that attempts to understand the pattern of particle physics and gravity in terms of an underlying structure with larger numbers of dimensions. One consequence is that there must be a large number of possible vacuum states, each with a different value of the cosmological constant – the so-called 'landscape'.

synthetic/analytic distinction Term of art that goes back to the eighteenth-century philosopher Kant and has been widely used by twentieth-century philosophers too, such as W. V. O. Quine. Analytic truths are truths independent of matters of fact, whereas synthetic truths are such in virtue of matters of fact. For example, the sentence 'all bachelors are unmarried men' is analytic as we can ascertain its truth in virtue of the meaning of the words 'bachelors' and 'unmarried', independently of matters of fact. By contrast, a sentence such as 'the Earth orbits the sun' is synthetic as its truth must be established by considering matters of fact, and not just the meaning of the words 'Earth', 'sun' and 'orbits'.

task-negative network/default-mode network A network of brain regions, mostly comprising cortical regions located on the medial surface of the brain (where the brain's two hemispheres face each other), which becomes activated when one is not focused on a specific task involving the external environment, but on one's own inner world – daydreaming, retrieving memories, or planning for the future. This network's activity is anti-correlated with the task-positive network.

task-positive network/fronto-parietal network/dorsal attention network A network of brain regions, mostly comprising cortical regions located on the dorsolateral surface of the brain (the upper-outer parts of the brain's surface), which becomes activated when one is focused on a specific task involving the external environment. This network's activity is anti-correlated with the task-negative network.

teleological explanation Explanation via an end, a goal-state, or a 'final cause'. Arguments that nature shows evidence of Design are called 'teleological arguments'. Natural selection can explain goal-seeking and functionality in nature without invoking Design or intention.

thalamus A subcortical brain structure that serves as a relay centre for information in the brain, and is involved in regulating consciousness through influencing arousal and sleep–wake cycles.

tired light A model suggested by Zwicky in 1929 as an alternative interpretation of redshift in terms of photons losing energy over large distances. Disproved most directly by observations of time dilation in supernovae.

trait A general term for any aspect of an organism's genes, body, behaviour, or knowledge. Traits could be socially learned, a reflection of the genes, or a combination of these and other processes.

transcranial magnetic stimulation (TMS) A non-invasive technique used in neuroscience research, in which a strong, rapid magnetic pulse is applied to the head, briefly interfering with the activity of the cortical region closest to the pulse. Observing how the pulse affects perception or behaviour allows researchers to reach conclusions regarding the stimulated region's causal role in the process being investigated.

truth In philosophy of science, the term indicates the ability of a scientific theory to be correct, i.e. to capture or correspond to the way things are in the world. But there are various other theories of truth, alternative to this 'correspondence theory of truth' (truth as idealized warranted assertibility, for example) and there is a debate about which theory of truth best serves the purpose of scientific theories.

uncertainty principle Heisenberg's discovery that the uncertainty in position (x) and in the momentum of a particle (p, which stands for mass times velocity) is in the form of a product: $\delta x\, \delta p = $ constant.

underdetermination of theory by evidence Term used to refer to situations where the available evidence is insufficient to establish a scientific theory over its rivals, since they are all equally good in accounting for the same evidence.

vegetative state A disorder of consciousness, in which patients are awake but not aware. Vegetative state patients have sleep–wake cycles (i.e. they may spend their days with their eyes open, and their nights asleep), but exhibit no behavioural indication that they are aware of themselves or their environment. The condition often results from brain trauma, stroke, or non-traumatic causes such as degenerative disease.

verification The logical empiricist criterion for demarcating science from non-science (in particular metaphysics) in terms of the ability of scientific theories and statements to be empirically verifiable. A statement such as 'Water boils at 100 degrees' can be empirically verified by boiling a sample of water. A statement such as the famous 'the nothing noths' by the philosopher Martin Heidegger cannot be empirically verified.

visual masking A method for rendering a visual image unavailable to awareness, by presenting it very briefly (often for under 30 milliseconds), and presenting a different image (the mask) in close proximity in space and/or time. In backward masking, a briefly presented image is followed immediately by a mask; there is evidence that despite observers' inability to report the first image, it may nonetheless be processed by their brain and affect behaviour.

wakefulness Being alert and awake and aware of one's surroundings; not asleep or otherwise incapacitated.

WIMPs Stands for weakly interacting massive particles. This is an example of a relic, where the dark matter might be contributed by the small fraction of particles and antiparticles that escaped annihilation when the universe cooled from an early hot period during which these particles were abundant.

zero-point energy An application of the uncertainty principle to any dynamical system that is capable of oscillating (such as electromagnetic fields). Because perfect rest is impossible, a minimum energy must exist when all quanta are removed. Thus, the vacuum should not have zero density.

Index